PARTY FABULOUS

12 PARTIES TO CHANGE THE WORLD

TODD MERRELL, JACK MILLER, and CAROLE NICKSIN

Illustrations by David J. Verruni
Recipes by Lee McGrath

Berkley Books, New York

Most Berkley Books are available at special quantity discounts for bulk purchases for sales promotions, premiums, fund-raising or educational use. Special books, or book excerpts, can also be created to fit specific needs.

For details, write or telephone Special Markets, The Berkley Publishing Group, 200 Madison Avenue, New York, New York 10016; (212) 951-8891

PARTY FABULOUS

A Berkley Book / published by arrangement with
the authors

PRINTING HISTORY
Berkley trade paperback edition / October 1996

The Putnam Berkley World Wide Web site address is http://www.berkley.com/berkley

ISBN: 0-425-15530-7

BERKLEY®
Berkley Books are published by The Berkley Publishing Group,
200 Madison Avenue, New York, New York 10016.
BERKLEY and the "B" design
are trademarks belonging to Berkley Publishing Corporation.

PRINTED IN THE UNITED STATES OF AMERICA

10   9   8   7   6   5   4   3   2   1

PARTY FABULOUS

Contents

First and foremost, *welcome!* On behalf of Jack, Todd, and myself, I would like to take this opportunity to extend an invitation to you to enter our world and make it your own.

Abandon all worries and judgments at the doorstep as you learn about our odd assortment of pastimes, rituals, and recipes. Partake in a joyous celebration of the moment.

Be *yourself* is our motto. Don't try to be how others want you to be. Be an individual, an eccentric. Be wild. Be fun. Feel free to do those things that you always wanted to do but were too inhibited to do. Now is the time; let us be your instigators.

Use this book in your own way. Most party guides stop after a briefing on food, drink, guests, and a little guidance on hospitality. Not *Party Fabulous*. We think you, the reader, need more help than that—because we *know* that we do. That's why we provide you with appropriate crafts, games, and music in addition to all the basics. Read through our book, then pick and choose the ideas, recipes, games, and crafts that appeal to you. Weave them together any way you want, or use our ideas as your inspiration for parties of your own design.

L is for *love*, don't you know, and that's really what it is all about. Love yourself; love your guests; love life enough to enjoy it while you're here. Think of each party as an opportunity to spread a little love and an opportunity to step out of the mundane and into the outrageous.

Out with the old, in with the new, out with the new, in with the old—mix it up and have a ball. Each party is just an experiment in living, a time to try on a new persona and create a little world to live in and share with your friends for a few hours. Think of your most outlandish fantasy, then turn it into a party reality.

Unparalleled joy is our aim with every party, and we're confident that you can achieve the same results in your home, too. Just remember the three key elements: love, laughter, and a couple of wigs. That's all it takes to have your guests exclaiming, time and time again,

"SIMPLY *FABULOUS!***"**

Most Fabulously Yours,

Aunt Carole

THE MEN BEHIND THE LEGEND

Throughout the ages, there have been many dynamic duos—Sonny and Cher, Batman and Robin, Ma and Pa Kettle, Adam and Eve, Adam and Steve, Steve and Eydie, Toklas and Stein, Olivier and Kaye, Jekyll and Hyde—the list goes on and on, a testament to the fact that two heads are better than one . . . or something like that.

And so it came to pass that in this grand tradition of partnership, Jack Miller and Todd Merrell threw on a couple of wigs and opened the Universal Grill, thus transforming themselves from the Laurel and Hardy of the food service industry into the Lucy and Ethel of lower Manhattan.

That was five years ago. Today the Universal Grill has evolved into a total dining experience, part restaurant, part sideshow. Walk in on an average evening and find a portly patron belly dancing down the aisle, or half a dozen people waving candles and singing along to "You Light Up My Life." And that's just the sort of controlled chaos they intend to teach you to create in your own home, with the help of the book you now hold in your hands. With *Party Fabulous*, the Miller/Merrell team pose the pertinent questions:

Are you adrift in a cultural wasteland, alone in a
postmodern landscape?
Do you crave a sense of family, a sense of community,
even though you deliberately left your own family and
hometown behind years ago?
Do you yearn for interaction with other human beings but fear that
you lack the skills to make any significant connections?

If you answered yes to any of the above questions, don't despair—just throw a party! In the following pages, this Stiller and Meara of entertaining will provide you with all the skills you need to be host or hostess with the most or mostess.

Whether your personal tastes run toward the dignified (like Todd's) or the decadent (like Jack's), you'll find that Miller and Merrell's basic tenets of entertaining—a sense of love, a spirit of giving and a willingness to play—will make your parties fly. Follow their example and give everything you do your all, and pretty soon it will catch on. Embrace the preposterous and turn it into something fabulous—something *Party Fabulous*.

Dancing Queen Surprise Birthday for Twelve

MENU
Universal's Famous Shrimp and Avocado Rolls
Pretty in Pink Tomato and Fennel Soup
Red Wine Poached Pears with Roquefort and Pistachios
Radicchio and Lola Rosa Salad with Roasted Beets and Goat Cheese
Think Pink Sautéed Salmon with Cranberry Chutney
Celery Root and Carrot Purée
Boiled New Potatoes with Dill
Grandma Champagne's Red Velvet Cake with Mighty Real Icing

GAMES AND THINGS
Mini-Roast
The Hokey Pokey
The Production Number

COCKTAILS
Cosmopolitan

CRAFTS
Picture-Me T-Shirt Invitations
Imperial Margarine–Style Crown

Once upon a time, when you were a wee little child, a birthday party was probably the first party you ever went to. You wore a sharp new outfit, played some games, gorged yourself with cake, and brought a swell gift you'd have rather kept for yourself. Maybe you cried because someone hurt your feelings, or because you were so jealous of all the attention that damned birthday child was getting.

Now that you're a grown-up, it's not all that different. You've exchanged Hawaiian Punch for something a little more potent, which is one of the up-sides of adulthood, but now when someone hurts your feelings, you can't call Mom to come and pick you up. You just drink more.

The Dancing Queen Surprise Birthday Party is an opportunity for you and your friends to rediscover the joys of childhood (like The Hokey Pokey) and combine them with the advantages of adulthood (like drinking Cosmopolitans and charging really expensive gifts on your credit card). Parties are a form of therapy for us, and throwing a birthday party for one of your dearest friends is the perfect antidote for too much time spent obsessing about yourself and your own convoluted life. This party demands that you obsess about someone else for a change.

Embark on the road to selflessness by *channeling* the Birthday Queen, and trying to intuit what will make him or her happy. Incorporate all the honored one's favorite things into the festivities: his or her favorite color, favorite music, favorite people, and favorite food. If you know that your friend harbors some unfulfilled birthday wish left over from their childhood, well, gosh darn it, fulfill it! Be it an Easy-Bake Oven or a Shetland pony, make it your mission to track down the object of the Birthday Queen's desire and have it for him or her on their special night.

Human beings are perverse creatures, which means that nothing is ever as simple as it could or should be. Placing all your focus on your friend while preparing this birthday bash might feel refreshing at first, but don't be surprised if it carries with it a certain negative undercurrent. As the designated day arrives, you might find yourself wondering what made you think you ever wanted to throw a birthday party for this person in the first place. This kind of thinking does not in any way make you a horrible person. You're just a little cranky, perhaps in need of a nap. And if that doesn't work, and you wake up still feeling a bit collicky toward the Birthday Queen, then it's time to employ one of the basic tenets of throwing a PARTY FABULOUS, and that is, "Smile, smile, smile—it's a lesson in denial." Be it nerves or fatigue, when the party hour rolls around, our unofficial survey shows that at least fifty percent of host/esses are not in the mood. Don't fret about it. It's just natural. The important thing is not to give into it, not to allow yourself to be swayed by "I don't feel like it, I don't want to today." Finish your preparations, throw some tunes on the turntable, and toss back a Cosmo or two. By the time the doorbell rings, you'll have forgotten that you'd rather be in your bathrobe, watching re-runs of *Hollywood Squares*. Think of it as a Zen thing, and perform the ritual for the ritual's sake.

Rituals seem to have gotten lost in modern-day life, and that's why we're setting forth to create a few of our own. Sure, our rituals are juvenile, perhaps even meaningless. But meaning comes from repetition, and besides that, the rituals we do are fun. Who knows? — in another thousand years, anthropologists may be talking about that strange tribe and their quaint anthem, "Dancing Queen."

So let the rituals begin the moment the birthday guy or gal walks in the door. The guests, who have arrived an hour in advance and who haven't breathed a word about the party to the guest of honor (hah!), will greet him wearing t-shirts bearing his image. "Dancing Queen" will be blaring and the tamborines banging while he is crowned with the IMPERIAL MARGARINE–style crown made especially for the occasion. Pass around a tray of cosmos and let the good times roll. Eat too much, drink too much, dance 'til you drop, and keep smiling. Just remember to honor the birthday guy or gal all night long. After all, your friend might be a tired old queen the rest of the year, but for today he or she is the DANCING QUEEN.

Picture-Me T-shirt Invitations

No need to worry about a fabulous ensemble for this party, because everybody will simply wear their invitation.

YOU'LL NEED

An assortment of photos of the birthday queen, ranging from birth to the present (You may need to track down the mom or brother or sister of the guest of honor to get those early shots.)
Twelve cotton T-shirts

WHAT TO DO

- Assemble a collection of twelve different photos (one for each guest).
- Mount each one on a piece of paper, and write the pertinent information (who, what, where, and when) around the photo in an artful manner.
- Take the originals to the local copy shop, one that does color laser T-shirt transfers. The copy man will do the rest. All you have to do is choose how to send them—mailing tube, envelope, small box—and that's it. Include a little note telling the recipient to wear the enclosed to the festivities.

crafts

Imperial Margarine-Style Crown

A crown. This is *the* Party Fabulous accessory. Andy had his tape recorder, Coco had her pearls, Judy had her bottle of . . . whatever, and we have the Party Fabulous Crown.

Crowns can be funny. They can be wig substitutes or just great icebreakers. Crowns can be anything you want them to be! They bring a theme together. They bring your guests together. And if you have your guests make them at the party (as we do at Easter), they get the guests out of your hair for a few minutes.

A multitude of crowns can be made from those basic items you remember from kindergarten: construction paper, staples, and glue. Many others from everyday items that have caught your eye like macaroni or tin foil. Whatever it is that starts you off on the road of crown-making, go with it. Soon you'll have mastered basics, you'll be dipping deep into the well of crown creativity. Before long, you may find that crowns have taken over your life.

For this party, nothing less than the mother of all crowns—the Imperial Margarine–style crown—will do. It's going to take some extra work, but you're making it for that very special friend, the Dancing Queen. She or he deserves a memento, something that will last, something made out of *foam rubber!*

YOU'LL NEED

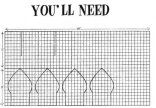

Two feet of ½" foam rubber (the foam will come 4' wide)
Scissors
Very heavy-duty string or yarn
A large sewing needle (the eye must be big enough for the string)
Medium gauge wire
Blue, yellow, and red spray paint

WHAT TO DO

Fig. 1

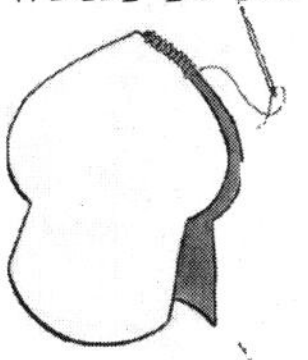

Fig. 2a

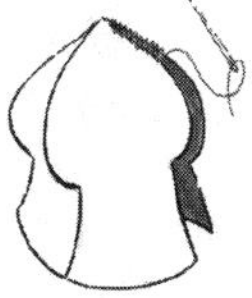

Fig. 2b

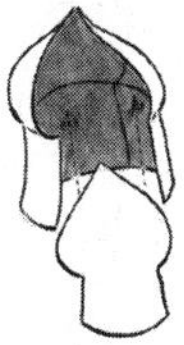

Fig. 2c

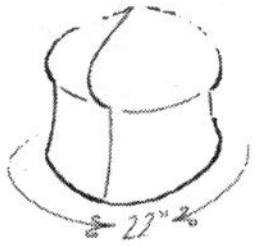

Fig. 3

This crown may seem daunting at first, but just go with it. Picture the end result. During the process, it will help you persevere through any difficulties. And if you do get stuck, don't despair, Miss Party Fabulous is there to help you.

- Take your foam and scissors. Cut the foam in half so that you end up with two pieces that measure 12" × 48".
- Using the first half of the foam, we're going to make the base crown by sewing four spadelike pieces of foam together. Outline the pieces on the foam (fig. 1). The bottom should be about 6½" wide, and the sides should rise vertically for 4", then curve outward and upward to a point. The width of the top is up to the creator.
- Cut out the spade design.
- Now get your needle and thread and attach each of the four pieces together, end to end (fig.2a-2c). It should look a little like a pointy mushroom (fig. 3).
- For the border, trace a rectangle that measures 12" × 26" (fig. 1) and cut it out.
- Now cut this piece so that it resembles fat fringe. Cut down, and leave 4" uncut at the bottom (fig. 4).
- Cut 4 pieces of wire 8" long.
- Take each piece of wire and push it through the center of each fringe section (fig. 5). (Are you following? I'm even getting a little dizzy. Let's break now for a drink and then we'll come back to the wire.)
- Basically, you want to make each fringe section pliable so you can mold it into a lovely arc. The wire gives it some heft.

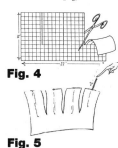

Fig. 4

Fig. 5

Fig. 6

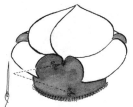

Fig. 7

- Sew the ends up 4" to the beginning of the fringe (fig. 6). Now you should have a lovely border that the mushroom thing will fit snugly into.
- Before you attach them, however, you must spray-paint them. The preferred color scheme is to paint the mushroom thing red and the border thing blue.
- Once that's done, attach them (use blue yarn or string) by sewing around the bottom and at the end of the cuts of the fringe (fig. 7). Almost done!
- Now you need a pom-pom for the top. Cut a bunch of little strips of foam, 8" long and ¼" wide (fig. 8a). Spray-paint them yellow.
- When they are dry, tie them up by first folding them in the middle and then tying the base up real tight (fig. 8b).
- Sew the pom-pom to the top of the crown, and it's done (fig. 9).

Gorgeous, simply gorgeous!

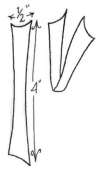

Fig. 8a

Fig. 8b

Fig. 9

games & things

The activities for this shindig are simple (like us!) but important. They keep the party moving and enhance the birthday ritual, in addition to being loads of fun.

Mini-Roast

Before the guest of honor arrives, have each of the guests write down an anecdote about the birthday queen. They can be funny and embarrassing or touching and poignant. If you're super-ambitious, you can even do some research in advance and have long-lost relatives send you their favorite remembrances of the birthday queen. Collect them all in a big fishbowl or brandy snifter. Then have a different guest pull one out and read it with every round of cosmos—kind of like a toast.

Miss Party Fabulous Says: If the anecdotes aren't that funny, choose the guest who is the natural comedian of the bunch to read them—and spice them up.

The Hokey Pokey

After dinner, get the blood pumping again with a rollicking hokey pokey. Just put the record on the turntable—the instructions are part of the song.

The Production Number

One way to honor the birthday guy or gal is with a great big lavish production number. You know, costumes, spotlights, a small orchestra . . . What? You think that's a bit over the top? Well, maybe you're right. But still, a group dance is always a good thing. Here are instructions for some simple dance routines that fall somewhere in between a chorus line and a football cheer. Practice them yourself, then teach them to your guests before the birthday guy or gal arrives. Ready? Five, six, seven, eight!!!

DANCING QUEEN: For this song, our dance steps are extra simple. Start with a basic sway, moving back and forth, banging the tambourine once to the left, then to the right, repeat repeat etc. When the words say "See that girl, watch that scene," put your left hand on your hip and extend your right hand (your tambourine hand) out to the dancing queen. Resume the basic sway until the end of the verse, when the music goes, "thump thump." At that point you'll want to do a double clap of the tambourine with both arms extended to the dancing queen. Do this twice (in accordance with the music), then, Quick! Grab a Cosmo! You deserve it.

basic sway

THE THEME FROM MAUDE: This one requires attitude—sassy, brassy, attitude. For a bunch of counts, just bang that tambourine vigorously over your head. Continue doing so til the words say, "Ohh, Yeah!"—for the "ohh, yeah," do a half circle dip, starting down and ending up (see illus. for full circle, then cut in half). Go back to vigourous banging, then pause when the music pauses, right before the chorus. With the words, "and then there's Maude," extend your tambourine arm straight out with a punch, and shake it right at the birthday guy or gal. Keep shaking for the four counts of that line, then bring your arms back over your head and beat the tambourine there for the subsequent four counts. Repeat 2 more times, (for each of the "and then there's Maude" phrases), then for the final musical phrase do a slow, sassy *reverse* ¼ circle, (that means starting with your arm over your head and ending with it in the birthday guy or gal's face), accenting it at the very end with another little punch, right when the music says, "Right on, Maude!" Right on, indeed.

sassy ¼ circle

THEME FROM *I DREAM OF JEANNIE*: This one is a little more advanced. First, and most importantly, get your hips swaying like a belly dancer. Okay, good! Are you sure you haven't done this before? Next, use the harem sway. There are four counts per measure in this song, and you want to sway right (one, two), left (three, four), while beating the tambourine once for each count (that's right, you're beating it four times per measure). Repeat, repeat, repeat, until the break in the music, at which point you FREEZE! GREAT! Now resume the harem sway, up until the second break in the music, where you freeze again. EXCELLENT! Now it really gets exciting. You're going to do three Full Circles, each one lasting a full four counts. This is where you can bring in a little Isadora Duncan, and really feel the music, go with the circular flow. Beautiful. After the circles the music goes "Bom, bom, BOM!" You clap the tambourine over your head on each "Bom"—once right, once left, then right, then FREEZE (for one count)! Alright!! Back to the Harem Sway, then another freeze, then, for that last little bit of music, (the little end tag), three sways, then extend both arms out to the Birthday guy or gal for a final one-two-three, bang, bang, bang on the old tambourine. Whew, that was FABULOUS!!

harem sway

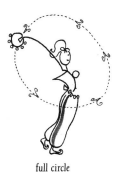

full circle

full arm extension

ABBA
The Singles, The First 10 Years
Atlantic Recording Corp.,
1982
"Dancing Queen"

Ray Anthony and His
Orchestra
"The Hokey Pokey"
Capitol Records, 45 rpm

Songs from Birthday House
Starring Paul Tripp
Fantasy
"My Oh My–What Shall
We Do With Our Hands"

Sheila E
The Glamorous Life
Warner Bros., 1984
Maxi Single

Inner City
Big Fun
Virgin Records, 1989
"Good Life"

Under the Influence of . . .
Love Unlimited
20th Century Records, 1973
"Love's Theme (Instrumental)"

Rosemary Clooney &
Prez Prado
A Touch of Tobasco
RCA Victor
"Cu-Cu-Rru-Cu-Cu-Paloma"

Sylvester
Step II
Fantasy, 1978
"You Make Me Feel Mighty
Real"

Debbie Boone
You Light Up My Life
Warner Bros., 1977

Je Survivrai
Regine
Carrere, Maxi 45T
"I Will Survive"

Mae West
Way Out West
Tower Records
"Twist and Shout"

The Peppermint Kandy
Singers
I'd Like to Teach the World
to Sing (in Perfect Harmony)
Peter Pan Records

cocktails

Cosmopolitan

As with any party, the first thing that guests experience is the most important, as it sets the tone and gives them that first hint of things to come. Hopefully, it starts guests on the road to oblivion—well, with this party, at least. That's because the first thing those birthday revelers are going to experience at this party is the cosmo! Or you can call it a cosmopolitan. Or you can call it nectar of the gods. Or you can call it high-octane Kool-Aid. Whatever you call it, you can mark my words: Your guests will be drinking them by the bucketful.

Anyway, it's an easy drink to make. There are not many ingredients. There are, however, other recipes out there, but this is the best and the most copied.

YOU'LL NEED

Lemon vodka
Rose's Lime Juice
Cranberry juice
Lemon twist

Let's use a 2 quart pitcher and that will allow us to make about 8 drinks at a time. Fill the pitcher with ice, and pour in ½ bottle of vodka. The pitcher will be ⅔ full. Then, pour in roughly 8 oz. of Rose's and a finish off by filling the rest of the pitcher with cranberry juice. If you want it a little sweeter, add a little more cranberry juice. If you want it a little tarter, add more Rose's. Swirl it around with the ice to get it good and cold. While that's chilling, rub your twists around the rim of the ever-so-chic martini glasses. Strain the

cosmo into the glasses. Oh my goodness! Don't you feel like you're in *Death on the Nile?* They just don't make drinks this color anymore.

Miss Party Fabulous Says: Stock up on the vodka for this party, because this is the only drink anyone is going to want.

Universal's Famous Shrimp and Avocado Rolls

This recipe involves many small steps that all come together to create a beautiful, delicious hors d'oeuvre. You can cook the shrimp and prepare the wasabi aioli the day before. Prepare the avocado relish at least one hour before assembly.

THE SHRIMP

2 lb. (16–20 count) shrimp
2 qt. water

Peel and devein the shrimp. Bring water to a boil. Add the shrimp. When the water begins to boil again, remove the shrimp and let cool. Dice the shrimp and refrigerate.

AVOCADO RELISH

3 ripe avocados
Juice of 3 limes
Salt and pepper

Peel and dice the avocados. Mix with lime juice and salt and pepper to taste. Cover with plastic wrap and set aside at room temperature.

WASABI AIOLI

1 cup wasabi powder	1 bunch of cilantro
½ cup warm water	4 oz. honey
1 egg	4 oz. lime juice
2 egg yolks	Salt to taste
3 cloves garlic	1½ cups canola oil

First make a wasabi paste by combining the wasabi powder with warm water. Mix until smooth. Mix paste with all remaining ingredients, except the canola oil, into food processor. When this mixture is smooth, add the oil in a slow, steady stream until emulsified. Keep aioli in refrigerator until needed.

THE ASSEMBLY

8 flour tortillas (8" diameter is best)	½ cup chayote, julienned
8 tablespoons wasabi aioli	½ cup carrot, julienned
8 tablespoons avocado relish	2 lbs. shrimp, cooked, diced
1 bunch watercress, chopped	1 tablespoon sesame seeds

Preheat oven to 350°. Place tortillas on a cookie sheet and warm in oven for 1 minute. Spread each tortilla with 1 tablespoon of wasabi aioli and 1 tablespoon of avocado relish. Sprinkle each with a pinch of chopped watercress, chayote, and carrots. Add 4 oz. of the diced, cooked shrimp. Fold in edges and roll up like a burrito. Cut each roll on bias, i.e., olive-shaped, into 3 equally sized pieces. Arrange on platter and sprinkle with sesame seeds.

Serve with remaining aioli for dipping.

Pretty in Pink Tomato and Fennel Soup

3 heads fennel, chopped	4 lb. ripe plum tomatoes
2 oz. unsalted butter	½ cup sun-dried tomatoes
1 carrot, diced	1 cup heavy cream
1 leek, diced	1 teaspoon thyme, chopped
1 celery stalk, diced	Salt and pepper
1 teaspoon garlic, minced	
2 cups chicken stock	
(see recipe, page 21)	

Set aside small leaves from fennel stalk for garnish. In a large stock pot, melt the butter. Add the fennel, carrots, leek, celery, and garlic. Sauté for 7 to 10 minutes or until tender. Add the chicken stock, both plum and sun-dried tomatoes, cream, and thyme. Bring to a boil, then reduce to simmer. Cook soup for 1 hour and 45 minutes. Add salt and pepper to taste. With a stick blender (or food processor) puree soup until smooth. Strain soup through a seive to guarantee a silky texture.

Garnish soup with leaves from the tops of the fennel.

Chicken Stock

10 lbs. chicken bones	1 bunch thyme
5 leeks	1 bunch rosemary
6 carrots	1 bunch sage
5 lg. Spanish onions	5 bay leaves
6 celery stalks	1 tablespoon whole black peppercorns

Add all ingredients to stockpot. Cover with cold water. Bring to a boil. Reduce heat and simmer 4 to 5 hours, always skimming foam off top, until you have approximately one gallon of stock.

Red Wine Poached Pears with Roquefort and Pistachios

12 small Seckle pears	1 bay leaf
4 cups red wine	½ cup sugar
3 cinnamon sticks	15 black peppercorns
1 clove	1 lb. Roquefort cheese
1 leek, chopped	1 cup pistachios, toasted and chopped

Peel pears and cut in half lengthwise. Using the small end of a mellon baller, scoop out center of each half.

In a large saucepan, combine all ingredients, except Roquefort and pistachios. Bring to a boil, then reduce to simmer. This should take about 25 minutes. You want to cook the pears until they are soft, not mushy. Test the pears with a fork; they should be done when easily pierced. Remove pears. Set aside and let cool.

Reduce your sauce to 1½ cups by boiling for about 45 minutes. Strain the sauce, set aside, and let cool.

Using the large end of the mellon baller, scoop a ball of Roquefort onto each half of pear. The Roquefort is easier to scoop when at room temperature. Drizzle a bit of wine sauce over the Roquefort and garnish with a generous sprinkle of pistachios. Arrange on a platter and serve.

Radicchio and Lola Rosa Salad with Roasted Beets and Goat Cheese

First we're going to roast the beets. While the beets are roasting, we can make the shallot-sage vinaigrette. Following are the three steps involved to create this salad.

ROASTED BEETS

12 beets
1 tablespoon salt

Place the beets in a saucepan, cover with cold water, and add salt. Bring to a boil and then simmer until beets are fork tender. Remove beets and toss them into a pan with cold water and ice to shock them. When the beets are thoroughly cool, rub them with a cloth napkin to remove their skins. Cut the beets into quarters. Preheat oven to 450°. Place beets on a sheet tray and roast for 20 minutes. Set aside at room temperature.

SHALLOT-SAGE VINAIGRETTE

¼ cup Verjus or rice wine vinegar
1 cup canola oil
1 shallot, minced

1 teaspoon chopped sage
Salt and pepper

In a mixing bowl, combine the vinegar, shallots, and sage. Whisk oil into bowl in a slow, steady stream. Season with salt and pepper.

TO ASSEMBLE	8 heads Lollo Rosso	12 roasted beets
THE SALAD	3 heads radicchio	12 oz. goat cheese
	12 oz. shallot-sage vinaigrette	

Wash and spin Lollo Rosso. Core and shred radicchio. Mix together in a large mixing bowl. Toss greens with the vinaigrette. Arrange salad in centers of individual plates, and garnish each with 4 wedges of roasted beets and 1 oz. of goat cheese.

Think Pink Sautéed Salmon with Cranberry Chutney

The pinkest of pink, this dish will have your guests breaking into songs from *Funny Face*. What's nice about this dish is that the cranberry chutney can be prepared in advance, and the night of your party, simply sauté your salmon.

12 8-oz. salmon fillets	12 oz. unsalted butter
Salt and pepper	3 cups cranberry chutney
12 oz. olive oil	

Season salmon fillets with salt and pepper. Heat a large sauté pan over high heat. Add 3 oz. of olive oil and 3 oz. of butter. Heat until this begins to smoke. Place 3 fillets in pan and sear on *each side* for 2 minutes. This will produce medium-rare fillets. Set aside in oven to keep warm. Wipe pan clean and repeat process for remaining fillets. When you're ready to serve salmon, place on plate and garnish each with a dollop of cranberry chutney.

Miss Party Fabulous Says: If you haven't already noticed, everything we're serving at this party is *pink*.

CRANBERRY CHUTNEY

4 cups fresh cranberries
2 cups sugar
2 shallots, sliced
Zest and juice of 2 oranges
2 cups Granny Smith apples,
    peeled, seeded, diced

2 cinnamon sticks
1 cardamom pod
1 jalapeño, split, seeded, diced
Pinch of Indian curry powder

Combine all ingredients into a large pot. Bring to a boil and cook until cranberries pop (about 30 minutes). Set aside.

Celery Root and Carrot Purée

2 oz. olive oil
15 cloves garlic
12 carrots, peeled, diced
6 celery roots, peeled, diced
1 qt. chicken stock
    (see recipe, page 21)

¼ lb. unsalted butter, soft
1 bunch chervil
Salt and pepper

Heat olive oil in a sauté pan, add garlic, and simmer at low heat for 25 to 30 minutes or until soft. Set aside. In a stockpot, combine all ingredients except butter, chervil, salt, and pepper and bring to a boil. Reduce heat and simmer for about 45 minutes or until vegetables are soft. Drain vegetables in a colander, but be sure to save the stock. Return vegetables to pot, add butter, and puree with a stick blender. Season with salt and pepper. If the puree is too thick, thin to desired texture with a bit of remaining stock.

Arrange on plates and garnish with sprigs of chervil.

Boiled New Potatoes with Dill

36 red potatoes, size B
1 bunch dill, chopped
1 cup unsalted butter, melted

1 cup scallions, minced
Salt and pepper

In a stockpot, place potatoes with enough cold water to cover and bring to a boil. Reduce heat and simmer for 45 minutes or until potatoes are tender. Drain potatoes. In a large bowl, toss potatoes with dill, butter, and scallions. Add a pinch of salt and pepper. Arrange potatoes on plates and drizzle with any remaining butter in bowl.

Grandma Champagne's Red Velvet Cake

½ cup Crisco shortening
1½ cups sugar
2 oz. red food coloring
2 eggs
2 cups flour
2 tablespoons cocoa powder

1 teaspoon salt
1 cup buttermilk
1 teaspoon vanilla
1 teaspoon baking soda
1 teaspoon vinegar

Preheat oven to 350°.

In a bowl, cream together the Crisco and sugar until smooth. Mix in the red food coloring. Add the eggs, one at a time, beating the mixture and scraping down bowl after adding each egg.

In a seperate bowl, sift together the flour, cocoa, and salt—not once, but three times.

Blend the Crisco and flour mixtures together. Blend in the buttermilk and vanilla. Dissolve baking soda into vinegar and quickly fold this mixture into batter.

Pour batter into two 9", lightly greased and floured cake pans and bake for 30 minutes.

MIGHTY REAL ICING

½ cup flour
1 cup milk
¼ teaspoon salt

1 cup Crisco shortening
1 cup sugar
3 teaspoons vanilla extract

In a saucepan, mix the flour, milk, salt, and 1 teaspoon vanilla. Heat slowly until thick. Remove from heat and let cool.

In a bowl, cream together the Crisco and sugar until light and fluffy.

Blend the Crisco and flour mixtures together. Add the remaining 2 teaspoons vanilla. Beat icing until fluffy.

Before icing the cake, make sure that the cake is completely cool, otherwise the icing will melt.

Miss Party Fabulous Says: Cakes seem to have a nasty way of slipping off the tray, especially when the server is inebriated. It's never a bad idea to have a little something extra by Sara Lee around, just in case.

Plan a Party

Food processor
Five tambourines
Mirror ball
Smelling salts
Turntable
At least one wig
Reams of contruction paper
Dustbuster
Welcome mat
Spotlight
Cocktail shaker
A dozen ice trays
Two dozen ashtrays, assorted sizes
Two dozen martini glasses
Corkscrew
Scissors, glue, and glitter
Can opener
Fondue pot
Condoms
Polaroid camera
The phone number of a liquor store
    that delivers
Assortment of credit cards

Fabulous!

Electric ice crusher
Liquid spot remover
Maraschino cherries
Garlic press
Assorted knives
Two-gallon stockpot
Your mother's sterling silver tea service
Stick blender
Ten-gallon garbage can
Dishwasher, either electric or human
Alka-Seltzer and aspirin
Pam
A supply of Kraft Macaroni and Cheese,
    frozen TV dinners, or a list of local
    restaurants that deliver, just in case
    things don't work out
A copy of *Party Fabulous!*

Pink and White Elephant New Year's Day Party

(A Hair-of-the-Dog Card Party for Eight)

MENU
Shrimp Cocktail
Dainty Dish Chicken Potpie
Spinach Salad
Individual Pineapple Upside-Down Cakes

GAMES AND THINGS
Poker
White Elephant Gift Swap

COCKTAILS
Hair-of-the-Dog Daiquiris

CRAFTS
Empty Box Invitations
Better-Than-Nature Tissue Paper Flowers

One nice thing about major holidays—Thanksgiving, Christmas—is that you can pretty much count on being depressed. When people ask, "How was your Christmas?" and you say, "Lousy," and they act surprised and ask why, just tell them, "Because it was *Christmas* and I had a *really bad childhood*," and they have to understand. Nowadays, it's almost uncool not to get depressed on major holidays. If for some reason something goes right and you don't get depressed, it's like getting an unanticipated present that you really like: a rare but lovely experience.

As bad as major holidays can be, they're nothing compared to the secondary ones: Memorial Day (ugh!), Labor Day (ouch!), Veteran's Day (yikes!), New Year's Day (put away the sharp objects!). These holidays have their own little way of worming themselves into your soul in the most insidious fashion. Maybe it's because you think that they're so insignificant that you don't bother making any plans, and then the day arrives and you suddenly find yourself in a paranoiac fit, believing that there is a secret party going on and everyone else in the whole entire world was invited—except you. It's too late to call your friends—after all, you don't want to let them know that you're home alone on a holiday. You're too antsy to stay home, but the worst thing you can do is to allow the allure of the holiday sales seduce you into a trip to the shopping mall. You'll end up with a suit from last season that you don't even like but that you bought anyway because the price was just so great. By the time you get it home, you'll have already realized what a pathetic mistake it was, which will make you all the more depressed. After a few cocktails, you'll find yourself making a desperate call to the Psychic Friends Network, begging them to tell you that next year is going to be better.

Listen, friend. Don't do this to yourself. Take a tip from Liza when she sang, "Life is a cabaret, old chum." Don't wait for someone else to invite you to a party. That's like waiting for the cabaret to come to you. Avert disaster and plan way in advance to throw your own misery-loves-company Pink and White Elephant New Year's Day Bash. Why pink *and* white elephants, you ask? Well, the pink elephants are what you might see when you have your first daiquiri at three in the afternoon, the day after New Year's Eve. The white elephants are what you'll be getting rid of, as all the guests will bring wrapped reject gifts or unwanted items to be used as prizes for the poker game.

Try throwing this party once, and it is certain to become a tradition. After all, you won't be alone, you'll have the opportunity to drink with your friends, and you can unload all those loathsome suits you bought on all those lonely holidays gone by on your unsuspecting guests.

**Empty Box
Invitations**

Since we're going to have a White Elephant Present Swap after the card game, the invitation for this party is going to be hand delivered in a beautifully wrapped gift box that each invitee will then use to wrap their white elephant. (Mailing is an option, but you'll agree that this is the perfect invitation for that personal touch.)

YOU'LL NEED

Eight gift boxes
One deck of playing cards
One glue stick
One sheet of pink poster board
Pink wrapping paper
Two-inch-wide white ribbon
One silver marking pen

WHAT TO DO

- Finding the right gift boxes might be a daunting task, so try to find a department store or specialty shop that sells objets (you know, oddly shaped stuff that mom would call knick-knacks). They generally have a variety of gift box sizes to correspond to their inventory.
- Become friendly with one of the salesclerks and then offer to buy eight boxes. The perfect size would be 12" × 12" × 12".
- Once you've done the legwork for the boxes, it's time to start the invitations.
- Cut the poster board into eight rectangles that measure 5" × 6".

- On one side of each card, glue on two of the playing cards in a V shape, using one face card and one number card.
- On the other side, using your gorgeous silver marker, you'll need to print out the information for the party: date, time, place, etc.
- At the bottom, you'll need to add two lines like this:
  "Bring one white elephant—either a despised Christmas gift or just something from the attic—wrapped in this gift box.
  "Also bring a bunch of pennies, because we're going to play some cards."
- Place each invitation in a box.
- Wrap with the lovely pink paper and tie with the white ribbon in the classic fashion.
- Finally, in each of the four pink squares on the top of each box, glue on a playing card. We want to make sure everyone realizes it's a card party, after all.
- Fill up the van with your boxes and set off on your deliveries.

crafts

Better-Than-Nature Tissue Paper Flowers

One of Todd's fondest childhood memories is of making these flowers. While the other boys were playing ball, Todd was fussing with Kleenex, pulling the layers to the center, trying not to rip the tender tissue, fluffing them up to look like the peonies that were growing in the backyard. He was always such a sensitive child.

YOU'LL NEED

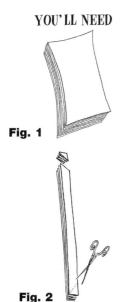

Loads of pink and white tissue paper (I'd be more specific, but who knows how many flowers you want to make.)
Scissors
White pipe cleaners

Fig. 1

The flowers can be made in a multitude of sizes from small like a boutonniere to as big as a basketball. Variety has always been the spice of life, so they say.

- Take eight sheets of tissue paper and lay them one on top of the other (fig. 1).
- Fold them in an accordion pleat: fold over, fold under, fold over, fold under, fold over, fold under, etc. with each pleat being 1" wide.
- Cut the ends of this 1" wide strip off at an angle (fig. 2).
- Hold it up at the center with your thumb and forefinger so that the folds face up and down.

Fig. 2

Fig. 3

- Take a pipe cleaner and wrap the top third of it around the center of the tissue strip rather tightly so that the tissue bunches a bit (fig. 3). The excess pipe cleaner will trail off the bottom and become the stem. Once the pipe cleaner is in place, it should look like a big, pleated bow tie.
- Gently pull the top layer of tissue toward the center (fig. 4). As you bring it closer to the center, the pull should become a bit tougher. Be careful; tissue paper is very delicate.
- Once the top layer has been pulled to the full and upright position, repeat with all the other layers on that side.
- Then, repeat on the other side. (This will be in our upcoming video, so don't worry.)
- When all the layers have been pulled to the center, it's time to fluff it a little, pulling together those stray layers, scrunching it to look more like a flower (fig. 5).

And now you're on your way to a beautiful bouquet.

Fig. 4

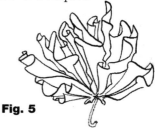

Fig. 5

Miss Party Fabulous Says: Alternate the colors of the tissue paper. Multicolored flowers are sooo exotic.

and

Decorate your serving table with a beautiful centerpice and make a stunning bouquet for the john.

and

Dab a little perfume in the center of each flower. No one will know it's not the real McCoy.

Card Party

Poker. Mention the word, and the images are always the same: back rooms, men smoking cigars, pizza, beer, and sandwiches; one guy winning all the dough and everyone else losing their shirts. Maybe that's why a lot of people shy away from the game. When you've got a game that's serious and involves money, people can get intense and downright crabby.

Never fear. We're changing all that. We're bringing poker out of the smoke-filled back room and putting it into the sunny, pink, front room filled with lots of pretty paper flowers. Now, get rid of the beer and whip up some delicious daiquiris, and replace the big money pots with beautifully wrapped white elephant presents. Isn't that nicer? We think it is.

To get everyone reacquainted with this time-tested funfest of a game, we'll go over some of the basic tenets of poker with a Party Fabulous refresher course. The first thing to know is that there are two basic games within poker: draw and stud. We like the name *stud*, so that stays, but *draw* is just so drab, we're going to change it to ... hmmm ... let's see, it's called *draw* because you discard the cards you don't like and draw new ones. Let's call it *relationships*! No, that doesn't roll off the tongue like it should. Let's call it *goddess*. There we go; stud and goddess, the two basic games of poker. Let's play cards!

Goddess Poker

The first thing about goddess poker that's different from its ancient counterpart, draw poker, is that the queen replaces the king in the ranking system; so it goes jack, king, queen, ace. That said, let's get to the game.

The game is five-card goddess.

- Everybody antes one penny.
- Deal five cards to every player, starting on the dealer's left, one card at a time.
- The player on the left starts the betting process. If he thinks he's going to do well, he'll bet a penny or more. If he doesn't want to take the responsibility, he'll pass, letting the person on his left take the responsibility, and so on.
- If no one thinks they're going to have a good hand, and everyone passes, the cards are given to the person on the dealer's left and this person becomes the new dealer. The new dealer must play five-card goddess.
- Once someone bets, then everyone either bets or folds. If they fold, that means they feel they've got a real crappy hand and don't think they can win.
- After everyone has matched the bet of the first person who bet, they need to take stock of their hand and discard those cards they think really stink with the hopes of getting really super cards that will make them win.

- After the crappy cards have been discarded and the new super cards have been taken in hand, the betting starts anew with the person on the dealer's left. That person bets what he or she thinks the hand is worth, probably a penny, and then the betting continues around the table, with people either raising (that means adding a penny or two) or seeing (which means just putting in the penny or penny or two, depending on what the person in front of you did).
- Isn't poker fun and easy?
- When everyone has met the bet, then everyone has to show their cards, starting with the first person who made the last highest bet. The best hand showing wins the pot.

VARIATIONS

Variations? How could there be? That was so fun! Well, there are. Wild cards! That's the thing that makes the variations so much fun. Or you can make people have a really good hand in front of them before they can bet. Like the dealer would say: "Okay, we're playing five-card goddess, and jacks or better to open." That means that everyone must pass unless they have a pair of jacks in their hand. Stuff like this makes the pot get bigger, but when you're dealing with pennies, I don't know if it's all that important. The wild card thing is more fun, because it makes everyone have better hands than what they really do. The dealer will say: " We're playing five-card goddess with deuces wild." That means that if anyone has a two in their hand, it can be any denomination: an ace, a queen, or a four of clubs to get that flush. The game becomes more racy when you've got those wild cards!

Stud Poker

This game must be played with cards that have pictures of naked men on them. Actually, the cards that disrobe when you put them in cold water are really fun. (Those are cards, not just glasses, right?)

Stud poker is fun because it's not as secretive as goddess poker. The other players get to see some of the other players' cards in stud poker. For some reason, there are two types of stud poker: five-card stud and seven-card stud. I guess men will always be size queens. As I've always said, "It's not the amount of the cards, it's the motion"—or something like that.

FIVE-CARD STUD

- Everyone puts in, or *antes* in poker lingo, one penny to the pot.
- The dealer deals two cards facedown, one at a time, to the players.
- The third card is dealt faceup around the table.
- Then the player to the left of the dealer (a Party Fabulous twist might be to start the betting to the dealer's right) starts the betting after he or she has taken into account all three cards in his or her possession.
- As in five-card goddess, if someone feels that their cards are crappy, they can pass or fold.
- After everyone has bet, the dealer deals another card faceup to all the players.

- The betting continues the same as before.
- Then the dealer deals the last card facedown.
- The players that are still in the game pick up their cards and then the betting continues in the same vein as five-card goddess. Fold or stay in.
- If everyone stays in, the person with the best hand wins.

Seven-card stud is very similar, only bigger.

- After the third card is dealt face up, the fourth is dealt faceup, the fifth facedown, the sixth faceup, and the last facedown.
- The betting continues after every deal as it did in five-card stud, only at the end of this game, you have seven cards from which to pick the five best.

Oh my gosh, we're having so much fun, we've booked the next Greyhound for Vegas.

VARIATIONS There are, of course, variations to this game as there were to goddess. Make cards wild. It always excites a game when things that are normally banal and lifeless become important and grand. So start the game out by saying, "five-card stud with one-eyed jacks wild." Oh, the tension. Another fun version is stud with your hole wild. Here, the wild card for each player will be different because the hole card, which is the first card that was dealt facedown, will be wild. Players bet as usual. Another variation is kind of like stud and goddess. It's called bet or blow. Five cards are dealt, one at a time. After each card is dealt, the person to the dealer's left starts betting without looking at the card. Everyone then bets in turn. After each card has been dealt, each player has the option to bet or blow; blowing means exiting the game. After the five cards have been dealt, the remaining players flip their cards, and the best hand wins.

Miss Party Fabulous Says: Here's a quick rundown of the hand rankings, starting with least important to best and I've given you some new names if you're feeling frisky:

No pair (me)
One pair (couple)
Two pair (kinky)
Three of a kind (ménage)
Straight (not in this game;
  we use the term *gay*)

Flush (orgy)
Full house (commune)
Four of a kind (oversexed)
Straight flush (porno)

White Elephant Gift Swap

YOU'LL NEED 8 white elephant gifts, wrapped in the invitation boxes.

- After the poker game, have each person cash in their pennies and give them a number that indicates what place they came in at cards (first, second, third, etc.).
- Then, when everyone has their placement, the first-place winner gets first choice of the white elephants, with the runners-up following in descending order.
- This is when the real fun begins. Up until now, the present choosing has been a grab bag. Since the gifts are wrapped, you don't know what you're going to get. But as soon as everyone has a gift, he or she can unwrap it and show it off. And now the trading begins. If you don't like your prize, you can start trading. A lower number takes precedence over a higher one, so if the second-prize winner wants your white elephant, and you came in tenth, you must trade with him, like it or not. But when you trade him, you acquire his placement, i.e., you get his old gift and his second-place ranking. So now you can make anyone who came in below second place trade with you—anyone *except* the original second-place fellow.
- Got it? Oh, never mind; just wing it.

cocktails

Hair-of-the-Dog Daiquiris

The image of Grandma comes to mind whenever the words *card party* are mentioned. Playing penny ante poker on Christmas eve and canasta on rainy Saturdays. That's probably why there's an urge to have a daiquiri when playing cards—because that's Grandma's preferred drink. Yesiree! Sitting around playing cards, smoking, and drinking daquiris; it doesn't get any better than that.

YOU'LL NEED

Rum
Rose's lime juice
Bar sugar
Shaker
Strainer
Limes

Pour 4 oz. of rum into an ice-filled shaker. Add 1 oz. of Rose's lime juice and a teaspoon of sugar. Shake and then strain into a martini glass. Garnish with a lime.

The Manhattan Transfer
Atlantic Recording Corp.,
1975
"Blue Champagne"

Guy Lombardo and His
Royal Canadians
Auld Lang Syne
MCA Records, 1961
**"Happy Days Are Here
Again"**

Marilyn Monroe
Never Before and Never Again
DRG Records, Inc., 1978
**"Gentlemen Prefer Blondes
(from original sound track)"**

Stevie Wonder
My Cherie Amour
Motown, 1969
**"Yester-Me, Yester-You,
Yesterday"**

Kenny Rogers
Greatest Hits
Liberty Records, 1980
"The Gambler"

Maureen McGovern
**"There's Got to Be a
Morning After"**

Chuck Mangione
Feels So Good
A&M Records, 1977

Authentic Sound Effects,Vol. 5
Elektra Records
**"Champagne Corks" and
"Sheep"**

Julius Wechter and
The Baja Marimba Band
Those Were the Days
A&M Records

Patti Labelle
New Attitude
MCA Records, 1985
Extended Mix

Antonio Carlos Jobim
Wave
A&M Records, 1967

Melanie
Gather Me
Neighborhood Records
"Brand New Key"

recipes

Shrimp Cocktail

This recipe and the ones that follow for this party are generous, in that we always expect more people to come crawling in on New Year's Day. After a night of reckless abandon, what better cure for a hangover than to be playing cards with friends and enjoying a simple homespun meal. Given that your hostess abilities may be slightly impaired on this day, all of these recipes can be prepared the day before your party.

1 tablespoon Old Bay Seasoning
1 gal. water
4½ lb. (16–20 count) tiger shrimp, unpeeled

In a large pot, add Old Bay Seasoning to water and bring to a boil. Add shrimp; let water return to a boil. Drain shrimp and immerse in ice water to retain color. Peel and devein shrimp. Cover and refrigerate.

THE COCKTAIL SAUCE

2 cups ketchup	Tabasco to taste
1 cup chili sauce	Worcestershire sauce to taste
1 cup prepared horseradish	Lemon juice to taste

In a bowl, mix all ingredients. Cover and refrigerate.

Dainty Dish
Chicken Potpie

Serve this dish in individual 10 oz. crocks.

4 lb. boneless chicken breast	2 qt. heavy cream
4 oz. butter	1 cup chicken stock
2 cups onion, diced	(see recipe, page 21)
1 cup carrots, diced	1 cup Idaho potatoes, peeled, diced
1 cup celery, diced	1 bunch sage, chopped
3 cups corn	Salt and pepper
1 tablespoon garlic, minced	Sherry vinegar to taste

THE FILLING Cut chicken breast into 1" cubes. Set aside.

Melt butter in a large, heavy stockpot. Add onions, carrots, celery, corn, and garlic. Sauté for 5 minutes. Add cream and stock. Bring to a boil. Add chicken and potatoes. Reduce heat and simmer for 45 minutes to 1 hour. Add sage and season with salt, pepper, and sherry vinegar.

THE ASSEMBLY Puff pastry
6 eggs
Chicken mixture

Preheat oven to 350°. Place one crock upside down over puff pastry and cut out 12 rounds of pastry. Place rounds on a sheet tray.

In a small bowl, beat the eggs and brush beaten eggs on each round.

Bake the rounds for 5 minutes or until brown.

Fill each crock ¾ full with chicken filling. Bake in oven for 25 to 30 minutes or until mixture begins to bubble.

Place pastry rounds on each crock and bake for an additional 3 minutes.

Spinach Salad

4 bunches spinach
1 lb. button mushrooms
10 strips bacon
¾ cup olive oil

¼ cup tarragon vinegar
Salt and pepper
8 eggs, hard-boiled

Thoroughly wash and spin dry spinach.

Wash mushrooms, remove stems, and slice.

Fry bacon until crispy. Let cool, then crumble. Set aside.

Mix the olive oil and vinegar with salt and pepper to taste. Set aside.

Quarter the hard-boiled eggs. Set aside.

In a large bowl, mix the spinach and mushrooms.

Just before serving, in a small saucepan, warm the oil and vinegar. Toss salad with warm dressing.

Garnish with eggs and sprinkle bacon over top.

Individual Pineapple Upside-Down Cakes

1 cup unsalted butter, melted
¾ cup light brown sugar
¾ cup pineapple juice
12 pineapple rings
12 maraschino cherries
36 pecans
1 vanilla bean

2 cups cake flour
1½ cups sugar
2 tablespoons baking powder
½ teaspoon salt
4 eggs
1 cup milk

Preheat oven to 350°.

Set out twelve cake pans (approximately 2" × 4" rounds work best). In each cake pan, combine 1 tablespoon butter, 1 tablespoon brown sugar, and 1 tablespoon pineapple juice. Place pineapple ring on bottom of pan; arrange 1 cherry and 3 pecans in center of ring.

Split vanilla bean and scrape out center of pod. Discard pod and save vanilla.

To start the batter, combine flour, sugar, baking powder, salt, and vanilla in a mixing bowl. Beat at low speed. While still mixing, add eggs one at a time. Add milk, and mix until completely moistened. Add remaining butter, and mix thoroughly. Gently pour batter into each pan ¾ full.

Place on sheet tray and bake in oven for 20 minutes. Top of cakes should spring back when you press in center.

Cool on rack for only 5 minutes. Run knife around edge of pans and turn out onto platter.

The Create-Your-Own-Family Reunion

(A Trailer-Trash Super Bowl Party for Fifteen Adopted Kin)

MENU

Shame-the-Devil Deviled Eggs
Crock-Pot Weenies
Lady Miss Bird Neighbor's Double Cheese Please Dip
Gutter Ball's Shrimpy Dip
Ham Boiled in Coca-Cola
Lumberjack Macaroni
Cousin Buddy's Tuna Casserole
Aunt Carole's Ambrosia
Hello Jell-O Pickle Supreme
Family Favorite Fluff Fondue
Auntie N's Dirt Puddin'

GAMES AND THINGS

Trailer Trash Scavenger Hunt

COCKTAILS

Granny's XXX High-Octane Moonshine Brew and a Pony Keg

CRAFTS

Hello Jell-O Invitations
Newspaper Pom-poms
Hi-Fi Potato Chip Bowls

When we were children, years and years before we all met, the three of us unknowingly shared a total lack of interest in televised sports. While our fathers, brothers, and even our mothers would whoop and holler in an uncharacteristic fashion over some silly game, we would sit in our respective bedrooms wondering where our *real* family was. "Someday," each of us thought, "I'll meet people like me, people who would rather watch the special on polar bears on PBS than tune into some horrifying game."

That day finally came. We grew up, moved to New York, met each other. Soon we met more and more like-minded people. We all grew to like one another so well that it just seemed natural to start naming each other. One by one, we christened a new fantasy family of faux-hicks, with appropriate faux-hick names like Uncle Rusty, Baba-Loo, Tyrone, Lady Miss Bird Neighbor, Party Naked, Peanut, Free Bird, Can-do, Gutterball, Suds, Daisy, Brown Sugar, Buzz, Ma and Pa, and last but not least, Cracker Cracker, 'cause it sounded so nice we had to name him twice.

Nowadays we're just a big, natural, down-home brood. We've been together so long that we have rifts and fights and this one don't talk to that one anymore kinds of things—you know, "If he's coming, then I'll be staying home." Just like a real family.

If you've ever wondered what it would be like to be a part of a family other than your own, the create-your-own-family reunion allows you to experiment with minimal commitment. Choose your guests carefully—they aren't just guests after all, they're your new brothers, sisters, cousins, etc. You don't need to match up DNA, you need only search for one common trait—a distaste for football. Because the one thing we don't do at this Super Bowl party is watch the Super Bowl (although we do tune in at half time, for all that fabulous singing & dancing).

The "Big Game" at this party is a scavenger hunt, a game that takes advantage of the fact that everyone else in America is at home, in front of the tube. Sure, you might antagonize some hulking football fan who misses the pivotal touchdown because you and your "cousins" rang the doorbell at the wrong moment. But try giving him a real big smile and telling him you're real, real sorry. Then mention that you were wondering if he had any old PEZ dispensers lying around. If he doesn't slam the door in your face, you may have just met the next member of your family.

Sports fans are always touting the bonding that occurs when a group gets together to watch the big game, but we think that's nothing compared to the bonding that takes place between a group of people who *hate* sports. You're with your people now, so kick back and let all pretensions go. This is a day to get back to your trailer trash roots, even if those aren't really your roots. It's a day to drink Jack Daniel's straight out of the bottle and beer from a bucket, and be glad that you don't have to feel guilty anymore about not understanding or caring about the all-American game of football.

Miss Party Fabulous Says: Just because you're dysfunctional doesn't mean you aren't entitled to have a good time!

Hello Jell-O Invitations

Super Bowl Sunday: a day to revel in big production numbers, all-American products, and men in tight pants slapping each other's butts. It is also a day to eat all those foods we grew up on: onion soup dip, Crock-Pot weenies, and Jell-O. And that's where we'll get our invitation—from the box of Jell-O. It's all-American food, there'll surely be a commercial for it at halftime, and besides, we can change the J to an H so it reads *Hello*—and that's just so welcoming.

YOU'LL NEED

A 5" × 3" notepad
Red and black felt-tip pens
Scissors
Fifteen boxes of Jell-O (3 oz. size)
Scotch tape

- First thing to do is write out the party information using one sheet of the notepad for each invitation. Fold into quarters.
- Cut 8 pages of the notepaper in half so that you will end up with 16 pieces of white paper that measure 2½" × 3". These will be the address labels, so now would be the best time to address them. Don't forget to put the return address in the corner. Set them aside.
- Cut out 15 pieces of paper that are ¾" × ⅞".

- On these little things, we're going to draw an H that measures ⅝" wide and ¾" high with the red felt-tip in the style of the Jell-O lettering.
- Before we attach the letter and the address label, gently open the box and insert the invitation.
- Now we can attach. Starting at the top of the box, attach the mailing label to the back side and bring the tape all the way around the box. Continue on down the box with the tape, making sure the H is in its proper place over the J.
- Once the box has been completely sealed with tape, all that's left is postage.

Newspaper Pom-poms

Although we've never cared for football, we've always had a soft spot for cheerleaders, and that's why we like to have these newspaper pom-poms on hand.

YOU'LL NEED

Eight sections of newspaper (about eighteen pages per section)
Colored tissue paper (consisting of the four team colors)
Scissors
Masking tape

- Use two sections of newspaper for each pom-pom.
- Take the first section and open it up.
- Take one color of the tissue paper and layer it between the pages. Refold the newspaper.
- Cut the newspaper from the top to the middle, leaving 3" uncut at the crease. Now, completely open the newspaper and lay it flat on a table.
- Repeat this with another section of newspaper, layering the team's second color between the pages.
- After you open up the second section, lay it over the first.
- Loosely roll the paper lengthwise so that the uncut part of the newspaper is in the middle.
- Fold the paper up from the middle, and tightly wrap the uncut end with masking tape.

- Repeat these steps exactly one more time to finish one set of pom-poms.
- Repeat the process two more times, but use the other team's colors.

And now you're ready to rah rah rah.

Hi-Fi Potato Chip Bowls

Everyone has them, stacked in a back closet or up in the attic. And what do you do with them? Throw them away? Give them away? Heck no! Make something useful out of them. Old, scratched records can become the conversation piece of your party.

YOU'LL NEED

One medium-sized metal bowl
Records
Spray paint (optional)

Fig. 1

- Preheat your oven to 450°. Open a window in the kitchen. Keep the air circulating while you're making your bowls; goodness knows what toxic substances were used to make these records.
- Place the metal bowl in the oven upside down, and then place the record on top (fig. 1).
- After a few minutes, the record will succumb to the heat and wilt over the bowl.
- Remove from the oven. Don't let it stay in the oven too long. You don't want it to begin to melt onto the metal bowl.
- After you have taken it out of the oven, flip it over and lift out the metal bowl (fig. 2).
- Allow the record bowl to cool completely.
- Now you may spray-paint and decorate it if you choose, or leave it as is.

Fig. 2

games & things

Trailer Trash Scavenger Hunt

Divide the guests into two teams, and give each team a map with the territory they can cover marked on it. Decide in advance how big you want the territories to be. If you live in the suburbs, you can make the area so vast that each team will have to pile into a car. If you live in the city, you can restrict the area to your apartment building, giving one team the even-numbered floors and the other team the odd numbers. That's all up to you. Make a list of ten trashy items, and give a copy to each team. Some suggestions:

A picture of a dog
A copy of *Highlights*
A Dionne Warwick album (these are everywhere)
A matchbook advertising something from a state more than 1,000 miles from where you are
PEZ dispenser
An airsickness bag
A reproduction of a Picasso (But if someone wants to donate an original, don't argue!)
One cat's eye marble
A FryDaddy, or any obsolete electric home kitchen gadget. Other good ones are the Presto Individual Hamburger Press, a large electric popcorn maker with a dome top, a Salad Shooter, or a Hot Topper.
A burned-out lightbulb

One of those purple Crown Royale bags

A total stranger (soon to be the next member of the family)

Set a time limit (an hour and a half is usually good) and you're good to go. Whichever team comes back with the most loot wins.

Sister Sledge
We Are Family
Cotillion Records, 1979

The Best Little Whorehouse in Texas
Sound Track
MCA Records, 1982
**"A Lil' Ole Bitty Pissant
Country Place"**

*Donny and Marie
Featuring Songs from Their
Television Show*
Polydor, 1976
**"A Little Bit Country, a
Little Bit Rock 'n' Roll"**

Joan Harris
Harper Valley PTA
Custom Records

Mrs. Miller
Greatest Hits
Capitol Records
"A Hard Day's Night"

Mrs. Miller
*Will Success Spoil
Mrs. Miller?*
Capitol Records
"Second Hand Rose"

Vicki Lawrence
**"The Night the Lights Went
out in Georgia"**
45 rpm

The Music from Marlboro
Country
United Artists, 1967
"The Magnificent Seven"

American Country
Capitol Records
"Running Bear," Sonny James

Ray Stevens
"The Streak"
Barnaby Records
45 rpm

Nancy Sinatra
Movin with Nancy
Reprise Records
"Jackson" with Lee
Hazelwood

Nashville
Sound Track
ABC Records, 1975
"Tapedeck in His Tractor"

cocktails

Granny's XXX High-Octane Moonshine Brew and a Pony Keg

What an afternoon! Good food, new relatives, good drink. Speaking of drink, we've got a pony keg out in the carport, but on Super Bowl Sunday, we want to get really loaded, not just bloated. Let's make that ol' college favorite: bug juice or swamp water or hairy buffalo or whatever you used to call it. And we'll keep it out on the carport so the pony won't feel so lonely.

YOU'LL NEED

One bottle of vodka
One bottle of gin
One bottle of tequila
One bottle of rum
Six cans of Hi-C

This is an easy one. Mix them all together.

Now, tradition dictates that it should go in a garbage can, lined with a clean bag, of course. But bags can be tricky. What if it is defective? What then? Well, we have a couple of alternatives for those of you, like us, who like to throw tradition out the window. The first is that old Coleman cooler. Clean it out and throw the punch in. It'll be like a liquid tailgate party. You can even keep it in the trunk of the car. The other alternative is actually our favorite. Put the punch in a gas can. New, to be sure. But go on down to the hardware store and find one of those nice new heavy-duty plastic jobs. Give it a quick clean and fill it up with the punch. One warning: Don't leave your real gas can in the vicinity. That wouldn't be pretty.

Shame-the-Devil Deviled Eggs

24 eggs, hard-boiled
1 tablespoon dry mustard
1½ cups mayonnaise
1 teaspoon white pepper

3 tablespoons lemon juice
10 oz. jar of sweet pickle relish
1 tablespoon paprika

Cut eggs in half lengthwise. Remove yolks and set egg whites aside. In a large bowl, mash yolks and combine with all ingredients except egg whites and paprika. Put mixture into a pastry bag with a large tip and pipe into egg whites. Garnish with a sprinkle of paprika.

Crock-Pot Weenies

1 lb. hot dogs
18 oz. jar of wine jelly

⅓ cup Dijon mustard

Cut hot dogs into bite-size bits. Mix jelly and mustard and pour into Crock Pot. Set on high until jelly has melted. Reduce heat to medium and add hot dogs. Serve when hot dogs are warm throughout; about 10–15 minutes.

Lady Miss Bird Neighbor's Double Cheese Please Dip

4 oz. cream cheese
4 oz. Roquefort cheese
1 tablespoon horseradish
4 oz. green onion, chopped
1 teaspoon cayenne pepper

1 teaspoon Worcestershire sauce
4 oz. mayonnaise
4 oz. sour cream
Sprigs of parsley

Blend all ingredients except parsley. Transfer to bowl, garnish with parsley, and serve with Ritz crackers.

Gutter Ball's Shrimpy Dip

1 10¾ oz. can Campbell's cream of shrimp soup
8 oz. cream cheese
1 4¼ oz. can shrimp bits

Dash of garlic powder
Dash of paprika
1 teaspoon lemon juice

In a bowl, combine soup and cream cheese. Add all other ingredients and mix thoroughly. Chill before serving.
   Serve with Bugles or Chicken in a Biscuit crackers.

Ham Boiled in Coca-Cola

You can get a ham from your butcher or use a good ol' canned ham.

8 lb. boneless, smoked ham
Water
Coca-Cola
1 cup cider vinegar

1 tablespoon cinnamon
1 tablespoon cloves
1 tablespoon pepper

Place ham in a large pot. Cover with equal parts of water and Coca-Cola. Add all other ingredients. Bring to a boil. Reduce heat and simmer for two hours.

Lumberjack Macaroni

2 lb. elbow macaroni
2 qt. heavy cream
6 oz. Dijon mustard

4 oz. Worcestershire sauce
1 lb. yellow sharp Cheddar, grated
1 tablespoon paprika

Preheat oven to 350°.
 Cook macaroni as per directions on package. Set aside.
 In a large saucepan, bring heavy cream to a lazy boil and reduce to 1½ quarts. Lower heat and add mustard, Worcestershire, and all but a handful of Cheddar. Add cooked macaroni to sauce and combine thoroughly.
 Transfer to casserole dish and sprinkle with remaining Cheddar and paprika. Bake for 45 minutes.

Cousin Buddy's Tuna Casserole

2 lb. elbow macaroni
5 6 oz. cans tuna
3 10¾ oz. cans Campbell's
 cream of mushroom soup
2 10¾ oz. cans Campbell's
 cream of celery soup

5 15 oz. cans peas
2½ lb. grated Cheddar cheese
2 6 oz. bags Lay's potato chips

Preheat oven to 350°.
 Cook macaroni as per directions on package. Set aside.
 In a large bowl, combine all ingredients except potato chips. Fill casserole dish and bake for 20 minutes.
 Crush potato chips and sprinkle over top of casserole. Bake for another 10 minutes.

Aunt Carole's Ambrosia

2 20 oz. cans pineapple cubes
1 10½ oz. bag mini marshmallows
4 11 oz. cans Mandarin orange slices

2 cups coconut, shredded
16 oz. sour cream

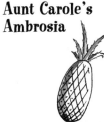

Drain pineapple juice into a large bowl. Add the bag of marshmallows to soften. Let sit for ½ hour. Pour off excess juice. Add orange slices (drained), pineapple, and coconut. Fold in sour cream. Refrigerate before serving.

Hello Jell-O
Pickle Supreme

4 3 oz. pkgs. lime Jell-O   1 cup dill pickles, chopped
2 cups cucumber, chopped   1 head iceburg lettuce, shredded

Prepare Jell-O as per directions on package. When slightly thickened, add cucumbers and pickles. Pour into mold. Chill until firm. Unmold onto nest of iceburg.

Family Favorite
Fluff Fondue

2 7½ oz. jars of Marshmallow Fluff   1 1 lb. box graham crackers
4 bananas, sliced   Assorted Chocolate Bars
1 20 oz. box peanut butter cookies

Partially cover flame under fondue pot and melt Marshmallow Fluff over low heat. Arrange all other items on a large platter. Dip items separately or create your own 'smores and dunk away.

Auntie N's Dirt Puddin'

1½ lb. Oreo cookies
3½ cups milk
1 12 oz. container Cool Whip
2 3.4 oz. pkgs. Jell-O French
vanilla instant pudding

4 tablespoons unsalted butter
1 8 oz. pkg. cream cheese
1 cup confectioners' sugar

Break Oreo cookies into small chunks. Set aside.

In a bowl, combine the milk, Cool Whip, and pudding mix.

In a separate bowl, cream together the butter, cream cheese, and sugar.

Fold both mixtures together, blending thoroughly.

Line the inside of a medium-sized terra-cotta flowerpot with aluminum foil. Alternately layer the Oreo chunks with the pudding mixture. You should end with a layer of Oreos on top, which you will need to finely grind to resemble dirt. Refrigerate at least one hour before serving.

Garnish by sticking plastic flowers into "dirt." Gummy worms are also a nice touch.

"We've Only Just Begun"
(A Valentine's Day Fantasy for Two)

MENU I Think I Love You Salad with Hearts of Palm
Universal Crab Cakes with Whole-Grain Mustard Sauce
Meaty Meat-Man's Steak au Poivre
Roast Asparagus
Baked Sweet Potato
Chocolate Fondue for Two

GAMES AND THINGS What Color Are My Eyes?

COCKTAILS Champagne

CRAFTS Be My Valentine Invitation
You Light Up My Life Luminarias
Mood-Making Table Setting

Due to our issues with intimacy, this is the one party we've never had the opportunity to throw. It's a fantasy party for us—our little gift to all you lovebirds out there.

If any of us had a boyfriend, we'd make this the most special day of the year. Kind of like a birthday party, in that you totally focus on the guest of honor, but with a twist of sensuality, a tang of the erotic.

Love. Love makes the world go 'round. It's a many-splendored thing. Everybody loves somebody sometime, and that love will keep us together, except when you must say good-bye to love. Then you find yourself thinking, *I'll never fall in love again.* But love may grow, for all we know. And soon you're saying, *I think I love you— but what am I so afraid of?* Well, love is strange.

In mythology, when the talk turns to love, death is never too far away. It's the same old story, whether it's Pyramus and Thisbe, Romeo and Juliet, or Running Bear and Little White Dove. Just at the moment when love is about to be requited, death intervenes, but somehow it's okay, because the lovers are united in eternity. That's real love—when part (or all!) of each individual must die in order for the new *love thing* to live.

For this party, first you have to define *romantic*, then you have to enact it. Todd, for instance, is a traditionalist, so if he threw this party, he might hire a violinist to serenade him and his beau. Jack's idea of romance is serving dessert

right out of the refrigerator, just like in the movie *9½ Weeks*. The most romantic couple in the world for Carole is Gomez and Morticia Addams, so . . . well, gosh, I'm not really certain what she'd do. You'd have to ask Cousin Itt.

Whatever your personal proclivities are, make this night a festival of the senses. Be sure you're in a sensuous mood to begin with. Take a nice long bath beforehand. Buy some love oil at the local witchy store and use some on yourself and save the rest to massage your mate later on. Listen to some romantic music. Wear some lounging pajamas or a nice silk robe like Hugh Hefner used to in *Playboy after Dark*. Go wild with candles, or if you prefer something slightly more sleazy, replace all the lightbulbs in your apartment with red lights.

Savor dinner, and make it part of the sensuality of the evening. Feed each other. Don't forget the aphrodisiacs—raw oysters, artichoke hearts, chocolate—they all add to the experience. Remember, love is the drug.

Valentine's Day sometimes doesn't mean too much to folks who are involved in meaningful relationships. It can get ignored in the hustle and bustle of everyday life. But for those of us who are single, it is a day upon which to pin all of our romantic longings. So please, at the end of your night of romance, say a prayer for the three of us, that each of us will someday have the opportunity to enjoy this party ourselves.

Be My Valentine

It's so hard to think of the proper invitation for a party of this sort. It should be whispered almost inaudibly in the ear or slipped inconspicuously into your loved one's fortune cookie after a satisfying Chinese dinner. But even though this is not a rambunctious party, we still have to stay in the Party Fabulous mode. So we're going to make a very personal homemade valentine to leave in your loved one's briefcase or slip under his or her door. Here are the basic ideas and suggestions designed to inspire you to create a completely personal invite.

YOU'LL NEED
One 12" × 18" red poster board
Extras, i.e., glitter, glue, lace, leather, feathers
Felt-tip pens
A knowledge of your invited
Photographs (optional)
Construction paper (red, pink, or white)
Scissors

The ideas for this ever-so-intimate invitation always begin with a big heart and a nod to our past experiences in grade school with the holiday of love.

- Cut the heart out of the red poster board.
- With the glitter and glue, start jazzing it up by putting on your main message (the main message is not the invitation info, that will go on the

back) which is, *I Love You*. Ahh, the romance of it all. This will be the centerpiece of the invite.

- Now, use the felt-tip pens to write any little cutesy words like a pet name or the date you met, stuff like that. At the end of making our creation, we are going to go over all the words in glue and glitter, but now we are just giving them placement around our heart.
- Fun stuff time! Attach things in all the empty spaces that remind you of your valentine, i.e., a matchbook cover from your favorite restaurant, a photograph from that romantic vacation, you know which things.
- Then, to finish it off, make a bunch of little construcion paper hearts and a cherub or two if you're really handy with scisssors.
- Glue these into all the gaps.
- Finally, border the heart with some lace or feathers, and your homage to the one you love is done. Oh—not quite—attach a small card to the back, which requests your beloved's presence at dinner on Valentine's night. That's amore.

**You Light
Up My Life
Luminarias**

With a dinner as intimate as this, who needs—or has time for—crafts. The concentration must be placed on the formation of a strong and lasting bond between you and your invited, on a perfect dinner . . . and on sex.

Mood lighting is always something that is at the forefront of a person's thoughts when planning an intimate dinner. That usually means candles—lots of candles. Candles are right, of course, but it is the way they are placed around the room that will make this party fabulous.

It's Valentine's Day, so let's make a bunch of luminarias (basically, little bags with candles in them) that evoke this theme of love.

YOU'LL NEED

Penknife
One dozen 4" × 6" bags
One dozen red votive candles

This is a very easy craft. All that needs to be done is to cut a stencil of a heart out of the two main sides of the bag. Once this is done, place the red votive candle in the bag and light it. The bags will glow with the image of the heart. How much more romantic can you get?

Mood-Making Table Setting

The main thing to remember for this party is taste and ambiance. Use beautiful place settings, a beautiful tablecloth, beautiful manners: I mean really, your true love might get confused that this is an MS (Martha Stewart) party, not an MPF (Miss Party Fabulous) party. Just to make sure that your beloved doesn't get confused, here are a few tips for some MPF Valentine ambiance:

- Scatter little paper hearts around the table and also the coffee table and the bedside table and any other tables that you have.
- Speaking of scattering, scatter rose petals over the pillows in the bedroom. They're very romantic.
- Maybe make a little altar to your beloved, which takes the idea of the invitation and runs with it. (On second thought, nix this; you don't want him or her to think that you have stalker potential.)
- No electric lights, only candles and a fire if you have a fireplace.
- Have a little gift set on your loved one's place setting; nothing elaborate, but it would be so sweet if you made it yourself, i.e., a scarf or cable knit sweater, if you knit, or a little needlepoint pillow.
- Lots of fabric gives a room a Victorian—i.e., romantic—feeling. Buy bolts of tulle and wrap your chandelier, use it as your top tablecloth, swag it around the doorways, drape or cover anything you can think of.
- Make a love mobile to hang over the table during dinner.

Miss Party Fabulous Says: Make sure the luminaria bags are completely opened wide. If they start to sink inward, you could have a mess on your hands.

games & things

What Color Are My Eyes?

This is a simple little question-and-answer game to find out just how well you and your partner know each other. Write down personal questions such as, "What is my mother's first name?" or "How old was I the first time I had sex?" on little slips of paper and toss them into a big brandy snifter. Have your lover do the same, while you're putting the finishing touches on dinner. Then, after dinner, retire to your favorite spot, be it the couch, the kitchen floor or a bed of nails, and take turns questioning each other. No need to keep score. You'll be keeping score automatically, in your heart, when you find yourself obsessing over the fact that your lover said your favorite place to have sex was in a canoe when everybody knows it's on an airplane.

Lou Rawls
All Things in Time
Philadelphia International
Records, 1976
**"You'll Never Find Another
Love Like Mine"**

*Ann Corio Presents How to
Strip for Your Husband—Music to
Make Marriage Merrier*
Roulette
**"Seduction of the Virgin
Princess"**

Marilyn McCoo and
Billy Davis, Jr.
I Hope We Get to Love in Time
**"You Don't Have to Be a
Star (to Be in My Show)"**

Carpenters
Close to You
A&M Records

Score Yourself . . . Sexual IQ Test
Gordon/Maxin Productions,
1972
Sample question # 64: "The
more educated a person,
the more likely oral sex
takes place. True or False?"

Carpenters
The Singles
A&M Records
"Top of the World"

The Best of the Stylistics
Amherst Records, 1985
**"You Make Me Feel Brand
New"**

Carpenters
A&M Records
"Let Me Be the One"

Rufus Featuring Chaka Khan
Ask Rufus
ABC Records, 1977
**"Slow Screw against the
Wall"**

Dean Martin
Everybody Loves Somebody
Reprise

George Maharis
Tonight You Belong to Me
Epic Records

Elton John
Greatest Hits Vol. II
MCA Records, 1976
**"Don't Go Breaking My
Heart"** (with Kiki Dee)

cocktails

Champagne

Romance. Romance. Romance. Is it only a dream? Not for everyone, only for those of us less fortunate. But in our lonely dreams, we make up intimate dinners, late-night rendezvous, and storybook endings. In the dream of a romantic dinner for two, the only thing that's being drunk is champagne. It just reeks of intimacy. In the movies people always drink it with arms intertwined or from a beloved's shoe. So, why break with tradition? We're going to drink champagne, too. But this must be Party Fabulous champagne. And since champagne is, after all, just champagne, we're going to have a Party Fabulous champagne bucket. Now, don't get all in a lather when you realize there's no spray paint or poster board or macaroni involved. We can be a little snazzy, too, sometimes. After all, we're talking about romance.

YOU'LL NEED
Two dozen roses with stems cut to 8"
Double-sided tape
One champagne bucket, 8" tall
One yard of 3" wide red ribbon

You can start acquiring the roses about three weeks in advance of Valentine's Day because we will need this time to dry them. As you are drying them, make sure that they are being hung with the stems up, buds down. We want the stems to be very straight.

Once you've got the roses dried, apply the double-sided tape to the base of the bucket. Then do the same around the lip of the bucket. The tape is not going to be what actually holds the roses to the bucket; it is just going to give enough stick until we are able to secure them with the ribbon. Now, arrange the dried roses around the bucket. The buds will be just above the lip. Once they are all in place, wrap the ribbon around the middle of the bucket and make a bow. Let the romance begin.

I Think I Love You Salad with Hearts of Palm

2 bunches arugula
1 head frisée
7 oz. hearts of palm

4 oz. tarragon vinaigrette
¼ cup dried cranberries

Thoroughly rinse arugula and frisée. Place in salad spinner to remove water.
Drain and rinse hearts of palm. Quarter each piece and set aside.
In a mixing bowl, toss greens with 4 oz. of vinaigrette.
Arrange equal amounts of greens in center of each plate.
In the same mixing bowl, toss hearts of palm with remaining vinaigrette.
Arrange hearts of palm on top of greens.
To garnish, sprinkle each salad with dried cranberries.

TARRAGON VINAIGRETTE

4 tablespoons extra-virgin olive oil
2 tablespoons lemon juice
1 teaspoon shallots, chopped

Pinch of tarragon, chopped
Salt and pepper

In a small bowl, mix oil and lemon juice. Add shallots, tarragon, and salt and pepper to taste.
Vinaigrette is best when made the day before and refrigerated overnight.

Universal Crab Cakes with Whole-Grain Mustard Sauce

½ lb. lump crabmeat
1 egg
1 tablespoon mayonnaise
Salt and pepper
¾ cup bread crumbs

4 tablespoons olive oil
Whole-grain mustard sauce
1 small tomato, diced
½ bunch chives, diced

Preheat oven to 350°.

In a mixing bowl, combine the crabmeat, egg, mayonnaise, all but 2 ounces of bread crumbs, and a pinch of salt and pepper. Once thoroughly mixed, form two equal-sized crab cakes. Try not to make them too thick. Roll crab cakes in remaining bread crumbs, coating evenly. In a sauté pan, heat the olive oil. Lightly brown each side of the crab cakes. Place in oven for five minutes.

While the crab cakes are in the oven, prepare the mustard sauce (see below). Ladle equal amounts of the sauce onto the center of both plates. Place crab cake in center of sauce.

To garnish, sprinkle equal amounts of diced tomato and chive around each crab cake.

WHOLE-GRAIN MUSTARD SAUCE

6 oz. heavy cream
2 oz. whole-grain mustard
Salt and pepper

delicious!

In a sauté pan at high heat, reduce the cream by half. Remove pan from heat and whisk mustard into the cream. Season with salt and pepper.

Meaty Meat-Man's Steak au Poivre

2 8-oz. tenderloin steaks
Salt, to taste
¼ cup cracked black peppercorns
2 oz. olive oil

2 oz. bourbon
1 cup veal stock (see recipe, page 76)
Pinch of rosemary, chopped
4 tablespoons unsalted butter, cold

Season steaks with salt, then roll in cracked black peppercorns. Heat olive oil in medium-sized sauté pan. For rare steaks, sauté for three minutes on each side. For medium steaks, sauté for five minutes on each side. Remove steaks from pan and set aside.

Drain oil out of pan. Keeping pan at arm's length, add the bourbon. The alcohol will flame and deglaze the pan. Once the flame has gone out, add the veal stock and rosemary. Heat until the sauce is reduced by half. Add butter (must be cold) and bring to boil.

Return steaks briefly to the pan, coating each side once.

Place each steak on a plate and pour sauce over steak.

Roast Asparagus

14 asparagus spears
1 teaspoon garlic, minced
1 teaspoon lemon zest

4 oz. extra-virgin olive oil
1 plum tomato, diced

Preheat oven to 400°.

Rinse and peel asparagus, starting from the base to within 1" of the tip. In a bowl, toss all ingredients, except tomatoes, coating evenly. Transfer asparagus to cookie sheet and roast for 6 to 8 minutes.

Divide evenly on each plate and garnish with a ribbon of diced tomatoes.

Baked Sweet Potato

2 medium sweet potatoes
2 oz. olive oil
2 sprigs Italian parsley

Preheat oven to 350°.

Thoroughly rinse potatoes. Rub potatoes with olive oil, coating evenly. Wrap each potato in aluminum foil. Bake for 1 hour.

When plating potatoes, cut on a bias and fan out on the plate, or cut lengthwise and pinch at both ends to create a pocket in which butter can be added, if desired.

Garnish with parsley.

Veal Stock

Prepare this stock on a day when you're just hanging around the house, hair in curlers, watching your favorite soaps and cleaning.

10 lb. veal shins
1 cup olive oil
6 carrots
5 large Spanish onions
4 cups red wine

1 lb. celery root
10 heads garlic, split
5 tomatoes
5 leeks

Preheat oven to 500°.

Coat veal shins with olive oil, place in a large roasting pan, and roast for ½ hour. Add all vegetables to pan, reduce heat to 350°, and roast for 2½ hours or until brown. Transfer everything from roasting pan to stockpot. Set aside.

Pour all grease out of roasting pan and discard. Add wine to roasting pan, place on stove over high heat, and reduce by ½, constantly scraping bottom of pan. Transfer wine to stockpot. Add cold water to cover everything in the stockpot. Bring to a boil, reduce heat, and simmer for 12 to 14 hours, always skimming the foam off the top. At this point, strain stock through sieve and return to pot. Continue to reduce (skimming foam off top) until you have approximately one gallon of stock.

Miss Party Fabulous Says: A good stock is a necessary staple for every party-thrower. You can whip up your veal stock one month or one week before your party and pop it in the freezer. Also, try freezing some stock in an ice cube tray to use in recipes that call for small amounts of stock. Just be careful not to plop these cubes into your next rum and Coke!

Chocolate Fondue for Two

1 lb. Calabaut or other high-quality chocolate, semisweet

1 pt. heavy cream

2–3 oz. flavored liqueur (optional)

Break chocolate into small chunks. In a double boiler, melt chocolate until smooth (about 10–12 minutes). Add cream to chocolate and whisk until thoroughly combined. If you want to add a liqueur, pour it in at this time. Pour chocolate sauce into your finest fondue pot, and set at medium flame.

Best served with a glass of fine port.

ASSORTED FRESH FRUIT

1 pt. strawberries

1 pt. raspberries

1 orange, peeled, sectioned

1 peach, peeled, quartered

1 apple, peeled, cored, quartered

1 kiwifruit, peeled, sliced

1 banana, sliced

6 ladyfingers

6 sprigs mint

Arrange all fruit and ladyfingers on a large platter. Garnish with sprigs of mint.

"Don't Rain on My Parade"
(An Easter Pajama Brunch for Twenty)

MENU
Smoked Trout Brandade
Blueberry Jam
Lamb and Ricotta Pie
Roast Pork Loin with Maple-Currant Glaze
Candied Carrots
Braised Endive
Bunny Head Cake

GAMES AND THINGS
Egg Races
Piñata Smashing
Bunny Hop

COCKTAILS
Blood Orange Juice Mimosas

CRAFTS
Springtime Baskets with Real Live Easter Grass
Papier-mâché Easter Egg Piñatas
Group Bonnet Making

Listen up, all you Party Fabulous hosts and hostesses. We can talk all we want about the music, food, themes, crafts, and games, but these things are just a means to an end, an elaborate method devised by us and implemented by you to trick your guests into having a good time and to get them to let go of all those silly, grown-up pretensions they've amassed over the years. Your duty is to use these tools to give your guests the time of their lives. A big job, yes, but we think you can do it.

Tool number one at this Easter brunch: bombastic papier-mâché eggs, of course. You might end up tricking yourself a little when you start dipping your hands into the flour-and-water paste and making these ludicrous but lovely orbs. Maybe you will find yourself humming, "A tisket, a tasket, a green and yellow basket," and believing in the Easter bunny for a moment or two. And when your guests feast their eyes on these brightly colored, oversized eggs, it will mark the beginning of their journey into a new and surreal world.

Tool number two: ask your guests to arrive in pajamas. Already, you have removed one protective layer from their identities. Cajole them into it, reassure them that it's okay. Tell them that Easter marks the beginning of spring, the resurrection of life. And what better way to begin life than in the same clothes that you begin every morning? After one or two blood orange juice mimosas, your guests will realize that wearing pajamas is the next best thing to being naked.

Allow the party to start off a little low-key, later breaking into gleeful. As the guests arrive, get them involved in making their own Easter bonnet. This is tool number three. Observe them carefully. Slowly but surely, each one will succumb to the power of craft-making. They will find that quiet place inside themselves that they may have thought they lost around the time they gave up coloring books. They will see that doing crafts as an adult is like being four years old all over again, with the added bonus of being old enough to drink.

Once everyone has their hat made—and on their head, of course—you can serve breakfast. Encourage people to sit on the floor—leave a bunch of pillows lying around and even a couple of blankets for people to cuddle up under. Keep the coffee and the alcohol flowing: coffee and alcohol together is like a nice, safe speedball. And keep your eye on your guests' progress, just to make sure that everything is going as planned.

Now comes the time to pull out the most secret secret weapon of them all: you. It is only through you and your enthusiasm, your *faith*, your commitment to the cause, that this whole scheme will work. Now is the time to give it one hundred and fifty percent. Grab the boombox, get everyone into a big conga line, and bunny hop down your street, tall and proud. It is your duty as a Party Fabulous host/ess to liberate your guests from their bourgeois inhibitions and help them find their true selves. Because deep down, everyone wants to be accepted and everyone wants to feel free to have fun. Deep down, everybody wants to lead the bunny hop.

invitations

Springtime Baskets with Real Live Easter Grass

Here comes Peter Cottontail, hopping down that bunny trail. And he's bringing lovely Easter baskets filled with goodies and eggs and lots of plastic Easter grass. Come to think of it, why plastic grass? Wasn't it real grass when Peter started his excursions so many years ago? Bet it was. And being the traditionalists that we are, our Easter basket invitation will use real grass.

YOU'LL NEED

Twenty small Easter baskets with a tight weave
Packing popcorn
Potting soil
Grass seed
Saran Wrap
Twenty eggs
One large nail
Fingernail polish, assorted colors
One sheet of paper

- First thing to do is make friends with your neighborhood horticulturalist. Not everyone has a green thumb, so having someone there to guide you along should give you some peace of mind.
- Layer the bottom of a basket with the packing popcorn. This will give the grass some drainage.
- Fill the basket ⅔ full with soil, packing it lightly.

- Sprinkle on the grass seeds so that they cover the soil.
- Then lightly soak.
- Drape the basket with plastic wrap and place in a well-lighted spot.
- The grass should take about three days to sprout. During this time, make sure the grass stays moist but not wet. There is the possibility that it can become mildewy if it is too damp.
- Once the grass has sprouted, remove the plastic.
- Again, keep the grass watered.

Now for the egg:

- With the nail, delicately poke a hole into one end of the egg. The hole should be big enough so that you could insert a pen into it.
- Now poke another smaller hole into the other end.
- Here comes the tricky part.
- Blow ever so lightly into the smaller end so that the the insides of the egg ooze out of the bigger hole. Make yourself a nice big omelette.
- Now, the egg is going to be very fragile, so all steps from here on out must be accomplished with the utmost precision.
- Rinse the egg to remove any remaining egg goo.
- Once the egg has dried completely, it's time to decorate, using the colored nail polish. Paint on scenes of Easter or just some stripes or polka dots.
- Once the egg has been painted top to bottom, give it a few coats of clear nail polish. This will strengthen the shell a bit more.
- Cut the piece of paper into twenty long, skinny strips and write all the party info on them.
- Roll up the strips and insert them into the eggs, making sure to leave about ½" dangling outside the egg.
- Place one egg on top of each basket.
- Put on your bunny suit and hop all over town delivering your invitations.

crafts

Papier-mâché Easter Egg Piñatas

Oh, that papier-mâché. You thought it tasted so good when you were a kid, a little like paste. It's kind of a shame that this particular art medium falls by the wayside as you reach puberty, but if you hang with us, it doesn't have to. Although we're not going to attempt (in this book at least) to make papier-mâché animals or plants or volcanoes, we are going to attempt the lovely, smooth and simple form of the egg.

YOU'LL NEED

Fig. 1

Fig. 2

A bag of balloons, assorted sizes
One week's worth of old newspapers
One 5 lb. bag of flour
One tin foil roasting pan (the kind hanging over the meat section at the grocery)
Half as many wire hangers as you have eggs
Assorted spray paints
Assorted poster paints
Electrical tape
Assorted goodies, i.e., chocolate eggs, marshmallow peeps, costume jewelry, lipstick, small stuffed animals, tiny bottles of liquor (preferably plastic bottles), a tiny book, a wind-up toy, religious trinkets, decals, fake tattoos
Ribbon
Two feet of twine
One mop handle

- First, cut your newspapers into 1" strips (fig. 1). They should not be too wide, as they will need to lie flat on the balloons when they are applied.
- Now, blow up your balloons. So far, so good.
- Let's make the paste. There is no hard-and-fast rule for the flour-to-water ratio. Just remember a few things. First, after you've put about a cup of flour into your roasting pan, *slowly* pour in warm water, mixing with your hands constantly. If you put in too much too fast, there's always the chance that you'll get lumpy paste or you'll make it too runny so that you'll have to add more flour and then run the risk of making it too thick, then add more water then—well, you get the picture, a 20-gallon tub of paste we don't need.
- Mix the flour and water until it has the consistency of pea soup.

Now for the messy part.

Fig. 3

Fig. 4

- Soak five strips of newspaper in the paste until the paste has become totally absorbed into the strips.
- Remove one of the strips by pulling it out, using your index and middle finger as a makeshift wringer, purging any excess paste.
- Drape the strip over the balloon and lightly smooth (fig. 2).
- Repeat with the other four strips.
- Try not to have too many strips soaking at one time, because they can glom onto one another or pretty much disintegrate if they are too wet.
- The strips will have the tendency to bunch after the first layer has been applied, so make sure that you smooth the entire egg after each strip is applied.
- Continue applying strips until you have achieved 3 layers of thickness.
- Now is the time to choose the two largest eggs that will become the piñatas. These eggs will need 5 layers.
- Since they must dry evenly, they must be suspended in the air. This is where the coat hangers come in.
- Unwind the end of a wire hanger.

- Pierce the tied-off end of a ballon that is sticking out of the papier-mâché with one end of the wire hanger. Slide to one side of the hanger (fig. 3).
- Using the same hanger, repeat, sliding the balloon to the other side.
- Rewind the hanger ends, fortifying it with electrical tape.
- Hang the eggs in a dry spot.
- The drying process will take up to 3 days and that should give you enough time to clean up that mess.
- When the eggs are dry, it's time to decorate.
- Use the spray paints as the base color for the eggs.
- Use the poster paints for the intricate Easter designs (fig. 4).
- Hang the eggs by tying the ribbon to the balloon (if it hasn't popped).

For the piñatas:

- When the eggs have dried, take the two designated piñata eggs and slice off the top (approximately 2 inches from the top), the same way you would if you were eating a soft-boiled egg.
- Fill with goodies.
- Measure approximately 1½ inches from top of balloon and pierce a hole. Make a second hole directly across from (180°) the first.
- String twine through holes and tie to form "handle."
- Make a ½-inch-deep notch 2 inches from the top of your mop handle.
- Hang piñata handle from notch.
- See "Games 'n Things" for how to play the game!

Miss Party Fabulous Says: Ribbon edged in wire makes the most scrumptious bows. They look like they've come out of a fairy tale.

and

Be sure all the balloons in the bag are egg-shaped; who has ever seen an egg piñata that looked like a kielbasa?

Group Bonnet Making

These crowns are the ones that will be made at the party. We're going to give you the instructions for three classic styles—the top hat, the turban, and the bonnet—then leave it to your guests to take the ball and run with it as far as their creativity will take them.

Top Hat

YOU'LL NEED

Lots of pastel-colored construction paper, 12" × 18"
Scotch tape
Pencils
Scissors (enough pairs so that every guest can have one)

- The base for this crown is simple enough. You'll start by making a stovepipe-like base.
- Attach two pieces of construction paper to make a cylinder that is 23" around and 18" high (fig. 1).
- Attach two more pieces of construction paper.
- Now take the cylinder and place it in the middle of the construction paper.
- Outline the cylinder's base (fig. 2).
- Now you'll need to draw eight tabs on the circle into the center of the paper (fig. 3). These will anchor the brim to the base. Also, trace the shape of the brim.

Fig. 1

Fig. 2

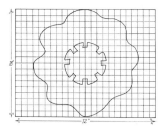

Fig. 3

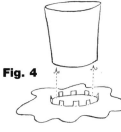

Fig. 4

- Cut out the brim, making sure to cut around the tabs.
- Fold up the tabs and place the cylinder over the hole (fig. 4). Tape to the cylinder.
- And there you go, the basic brimmed hat is done.
- Now comes the decorating part, and there are many ways to make every one a personal Easter statement. Make the cylinder part a different height. Cover it with paper flowers. Make stripes. Make it plaid. The brim can also be cut into different shapes and sizes. Scallop the edges or make the brim very large like a big sun hat. The possibilities are truly endless.

Turban

This crown is dramatic. There is almost an Egyptian quality to it: think Isis or Nefertiti.

YOU'LL NEED

Two sheets of construction paper, 12" × 18"
Stapler
One mediun to small tissue paper flower (See instructions for making one on page 33.)

- Fold the pieces of construction paper lenghtwise so that they measure 6" × 18".
- Staple one end of the first to one end of the second. Now you have a long piece of constuction paper that measures 6" × 36".
- Using your own head as the form, and placing the seam at the back of your head, bring the ends around to the front of your head with an upswing so that the ends cross each other perpendicularly.
- When the crown feels snug, and while continuing to hold the ends in place, take it off your head and staple it together.
- Attach the flower to the center peak.

Miss Party Fabulous Says: If the flower makes the crown a little front heavy, tape three or four pennies to the back seam as a counterweight.

Easter Baby Bonnet

This crown is for people having a bad hair day or who like to have their entire head covered.

YOU'LL NEED

Two sheets of 12" × 18" construction paper
Scissors
Scotch tape
Four feet of ribbon
Stapler

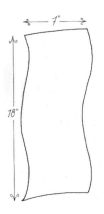

Fig. 1

- Take one piece of the construction paper and cut it to measure 7" × 18" (figure 1).
- Discard the other piece into your scrap paper bin.
- On the second sheet, outline the pieces for the brim and the back using figure 2 as your guide (remember one square is one square inch).
- After you have cut out the pieces, fold the notches to a right angle.
- Curve the rectangular sheet and attach the back of the hat to it by taping the notches on the inside.
- Do the same with the brim (figure 3).
- Cut the ribbon in half, and staple one end of each piece to the bottom of the bonnet.

And there you have it; an Easter baby bonnet.

Miss Party Fabulous Says: Decorate the brim with glitter or small paper flowers to spice it up.

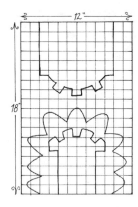

Fig. 2

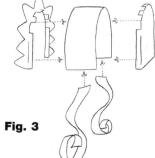

Fig. 3

games & things

Egg Races

This is just a simple race where each racer puts an egg in a tablespoon and, holding the spoon with his or her mouth, tries to reach the finish line first, without dropping the egg. Once you drop it, you're out. You better use hard-boiled eggs or else you'll ruin that valuable oriental rug.

Piñata Smashing

Those lovely papier-mâché eggs you spent all week making are about to be destroyed! Give one guest the filled piñata hanging from a mop handle. Then blindfold another guest, and spin them around. Hand them the other mop handle, then let them start whacking, aiming for the egg. The other guests can "egg" them on, shouting clues as to which way to go. Give each guest sixty seconds to try his skill. Once the piñata is broken, all the guests can scramble for their share of goodies. Caution: Remember not to play this game too close to your special crystal chandelier!

Bunny Hop

The bunny hop is an infectious little tune. The recurring "thump, thump, thump" provides a framework for a conga line dance. You strut for three bars, then do the three-hop refrain—easy as pie.

We've been bunny hopping for years. Just get your pajama-and-hat-clad party-goers in a conga line and either blast the song so loud you can hear it in your front yard or carry it along on a boombox. The rhythm is so easy to pick up that it doesn't even matter too much if you bunny hop right out of hearing range. Do a few bars to get you going, then it's straight out the front door and down the street. If you're feeling particularly springish and frisky, bunny hop right through the neighbor's front door—without even knocking.

Ray Anthony
"The Bunny Hop"
Capitol Records
45 rpm

Edwin Hawkins Singers
Oh Happy Day
Emus Records, 1978

Tom Jones
Live at Caesars Palace
Parrot
"Resurrection Shuffle"

Oklahoma! Sound Track
Capitol
**"Oh What a Beautiful
Mornin' "**

Saturday Night Fever
Sound Track
RSO Records, 1977
"Stayin' Alive"

Aretha Franklin
Aretha's Gold
Atlantic Recording Corp.,
1969
"I Say a Little Prayer"

*Happiness Is Being with
the Spinners*
Atlantic Recording Corp.,
1976
"The Rubberband Man"

Jefferson Airplane
Surrealistic Pillow
RCA, 1967
"White Rabbit"

Petula Clark
I Know a Place
Warner Bros.
"Dancing in the Street"

Godspell
Sound Track
Bell Records

Dolly Parton
Here You Come Again
RCA, 1977

Neil Diamond
His 12 Greatest Hits
MCA Records
**"Brother Love's Traveling
Salvation Show"**

The 5th Dimension
Greatest Hits
Soul City
"Aquarius/Let the Sunshine"

The Monkees
Greatest Hits
Arista Records, 1976
"I'm a Believer"

cocktails

Blood Orange Juice Mimosas

Easter . . . spring . . . brunch . . . cocktail . . . mimosa! It's just the natural progression of logic.

But our little mimosa has a new look. It's red!

YOU'LL NEED

About a case of blood oranges
A juicer
One case of champagne

First you'll need to juice the blood oranges, but don't juice them all. Save a couple on the side to use for garnish. The ratio of champagne to orange juice should be about three to one. Slice up the blood oranges that were left aside into half wheels and plop them on the side of the glasses. Fill the glasses up with bubbly and then with the ruby-red juice, and your pajama brunch is ready to go.

recipes

Smoked Trout Brandade

1 Idaho potato
5 smoked trout fillets
2 cloves garlic, peeled
1 cup olive oil

1 cup heavy cream
Salt and pepper
Chives, chopped

Peel potato, rinse, slice, and boil. In a food processor combine all ingredients, except chives. Puree at lowest possible speed, as you want to prevent the cream from whipping. Season with salt and pepper. Garnish with chives.

Serve as a spread with toasted bagels.

Prepare this recipe the day before your party.

Blueberry Jam

3 pints blueberries
2 tablespoons lemon juice
5¼ cups sugar

¾ cup water
1 box pectin

Rinse blueberries, remove stems and crush. Mix berries with sugar and set aside. In a saucepan combine water and pectin, bring to a boil stirring constantly, and boil for one minute.

Pour pectin mixture over berries and stir constantly until sugar is dissolved. Transfer jam to a container with lid, seal and let sit at room temperature overnight.

Serve with buttered toast and English muffins.

Lamb and Ricotta Pie

A delicious alternative to scrambled eggs. You can save yourself some time and prepare the lamb the day before.

THE LAMB

10 lamb shanks
1 Spanish onion, diced

1 carrot, diced
2 stalks celery, diced

Place the lamb in a large stockpot with enough water to cover. Add the onions, carrots, and celery. Simmer over medium heat—do not boil—for 3½ to 4 hours. Remove shanks and let cool. Take meat off bones and dice. Wrap and refrigerate overnight.

THE ASSEMBLY

1 Spanish onion, diced
2 oz. unsalted butter
1 qt. milk
16 eggs

1 qt. whole-milk ricotta
1 bunch thyme, chopped
Salt and pepper

Preheat oven to 350°. In a sauté pan, heat butter until it starts to brown. Add onions and sauté for 5 to 7 minutes or until tender. Set aside and let cool. In a large bowl, combine lamb with onions, milk, eggs, ricotta, and thyme. Add a generous pinch of salt and pepper.

Lightly oil three 10" cast-iron skillets (or deep-dish pie pans). Fill these evenly and only ¾ full. Place the skillets in the oven on a sheet tray ¾ full of water. Bake in oven for 1½ hours. Keep an eye on water in sheet tray; add more if it begins to evaporate.

Since every oven is different, you should check the pies after 1 hour. If you put a knife in center of pie and it comes out clean, the pies are done.

Roast Pork Loin with Maple-Currant Glaze

2 oz. olive oil
3 leeks, sliced
2 carrots, sliced
1 Spanish onion, sliced

2 cups maple syrup
3 qt. veal stock (see recipe on page 76)
Salt and pepper
2 cups dried black currants

THE GLAZE In a large saucepan, heat the olive oil and sauté the leeks, carrots, and onion for 5 to 7 minutes or until tender. Add maple syrup. Reduce by ¾ over medium heat. Add veal stock. Reduce by ⅓ over medium heat. Strain through sieve and season with salt and pepper. Add dried black currants.

ROASTING THE PORK LOIN 10 lb. boneless center cut pork loin
Maple-currant glaze

Preheat oven to 350°. Place pork loin in roasting pan. Ladle 4 oz. of glaze over pork. Roast for 45 minutes, basting every 5 minutes with 4 oz. of glaze. Slice pork, arrange on platter, and serve with any remaining glaze.

Candied Carrots

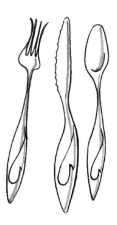

½ gal. water
1 teaspoon salt
2½ lb. carrots, peeled, julienned
Juice of 2 oranges
½ cup sugar

2 cloves
¼ lb. unsalted butter
Salt and pepper
1 bunch mint, chopped

In a large saucepan, bring water to a boil and add salt. Add carrots and boil for about 5 minutes or until tender. Drain and set aside.

In a sauté pan, combine orange juice and sugar. Stir over low heat until mixture starts to caramelize (about 5 to 6 minutes). Add cloves and butter, stirring continuously until smooth and thick. In a bowl, combine carrots with sauce, add salt and pepper to taste, and toss with chopped mint.

Braised Endive

1½ cups chicken stock
  (see recipe on page 21)
3 oz. unsalted butter
1 teaspoon black peppercorns, whole

1 bay leaf
10 Belgian endive
Salt and pepper

Preheat oven to 350°.

Combine chicken stock, butter, peppercorns, and bay leaf in a saucepan and bring to a boil.

Lay endive flat in a roasting pan and cover with stock. Cover pan with aluminum foil and braise for 45 minutes. Set aside.

In a small saucepan, reduce by ½ the remaining stock from the roasting pan. Remove endive from pan and cut in half lengthwise. Arrange endive on a large platter and drizzle with reduced stock. Add salt and pepper to taste.

Bunny Head Cake

THE CAKE

1½ cups sugar
½ cup Crisco shortening
2 eggs, beaten
3 cups cake flour, sifted

3 teaspoons baking powder
½ teaspoon salt
1 cup milk
1 teaspoon vanilla

Preheat oven to 350°.

In a bowl, cream together the sugar and Crisco. Add beaten eggs. Set aside.

Sift together the flour, baking powder, and salt. Set aside.

While continuously beating, alternately add flour mixture, milk, and vanilla to shortening mixture.

Line the bottoms of two 9" round cake pans with baking paper. Pour batter into pans ¾ full. Bake for 30 minutes. Let cakes cool in pans for 10 minutes, then remove cakes from pans and finish cooling on racks.

THE ICING   Zest of 2 oranges   2 tablespoons unsalted butter
                6 tablespoons orange juice   Confectioners' sugar
                2 tablespoons lemon juice

In a saucepan, combine all ingredients except confectioners' sugar. Over low heat, stir mixture until butter is melted. Slowly add sugar, stirring constantly, until icing is the consistency of heavy cream. Let cool for about 10 minutes before spreading on cake.

THE ASSEMBLY   2 cups coconut, shredded   Licorice laces
                   Food coloring, assorted   Gumdrops
                   M&M's, plain and peanut

Use one cake round for the bunny face. Cut remaining round into whatever shapes strike your fancy: bunny ears, top hat, bow tie, earrings, antenna, or a combination thereof. Ice all parts of bunny head and stick them together. Use the assorted food colorings to dye some or all of the coconut. Sprinkle coconut over cake and decorate with candy. Our cake looked more like an Easter Owl, but it was pretty to look at and fun to make!

Mother's Day Group Therapy Party

(A Don't-Forget-to-Bring-Your-Prozac Get-Together for Eight)

MENU Compose Yourself Asparagus and Shrimp Soup
Chicken Club Sandwiches
Pure Contentment Almond–Sour Cream Cheesecake
Sugar-Rush Chocolate-Pistachio Clusters
Lemon/Orange/Poppy Seed Cookies

GAMES AND THINGS "My Childhood Was Sooo Bad . . ." Telephone Game
Who Am I?
Ketchup Rorschach Tests

COCKTAILS Mother's Milk White Russians Served in Baby Bottles

CRAFTS TV Screen Invitations
Sanitorium-Style Popsicle Stick Trivets
Macramé Plant Hangers
Physical Therapy Basket Weaving

We know you love your mother. We love our mothers, too. It's just that sometimes, well, they get on our nerves. They push our buttons. We want to be good sons and daughters, but somehow we never quite measure up. Nothing we do is ever good enough. Mom is always talking about her friends' sons and daughters: "So-and-so's son sent her to Hawaii for two and a half weeks!" "So-and-so's daughter married this fabulously wealthy prince and they're about to have their third child!" "So-and-so's kids are all doctors!" It just goes on and on, until any good will you had toward old Mom has evaporated and you've been reduced to a whining, ranting teenager. "Can't you see I'm doing the best I can?" you find yourself screaming over dinner at Mommy's favorite restaurant. And then Mommy starts weeping, you feel like a bomb just went off in your chest . . . and it's Mother's Day, and you really wanted it to be special.

This party is so all your friends have a place to go after the Mother's Day ritual is over. A safe place, a supportive place, where you can share your feelings, put everything in perspective, and pull yourself back together again. We think of this party as an informal twelve-step meeting, and that's why we serve a lot of coffee and sweets—but have the alcohol on hand, too. When the gang arrives, all depressed, administer a quick sugar rush of cookies and candies. Then, when they crash from that, pronto! Coffee rush! When they come swooping down from that, get busy with the liquor binge!

But it's not just the mood alterers that make this party, it's the camaraderie you feel when you find out one of your acquaintances had a worse childhood than you did. The two of you will bond immediately, bond in your pain, and pain is one of the strongest bonding agents known to man. Pain is stronger than Krazy Glue.

Oh, let's not be so depressed. Let's have fun now. Have everybody tell their worst childhood memory, while one guest acts as the facilitator and asks, "And how did that make you feel?" Have a pile of stuffed animals for people to hold on to while they get in touch with their inner childhood. Play tapes of John Bradshaw on the VCR. Have lots of group hugs, and a few group screams. The party is over when everyone feels purged and rejuvenated, and ready to call Mommy in the morning and start all over again.

Miss Party Fabulous Says: Parties are like therapy for those who have shunned traditional analysis in favor of alcoholism.

invitations

TV Screen Invitations

We have a secret: this invitation doesn't really have anything to do with Mother's Day—unless of course there's some secret psychological link-up we've missed. But it's an adorable idea, anyway, and if, while you're threading the register tape through the little cigarette boxes, you have a revelation about the hidden subconscious connection between our little invitations and our warped psyches, be sure and let us know.

YOU'LL NEED

One ¼" dowel, 4' long
One roll of cash register tape 1⅝" wide
Eight empty cigarette packs (hard)
Penknife
Felt-tip pen
Scotch tape

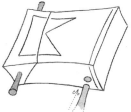

Fig. 1

- First, cut the dowel into 16 lengths measuring 3" each.
- Next, cut 8 lengths of cash register tape one yard long. Now we can tackle the assembly.
- On both sides of cigarette pack make two small holes ⅜" from each end.
- Push a piece of dowel through one hole and out the other (fig. 1). It should be snug. Repeat with other holes.
- We are going to make two incisions on the back of the box directly over where the dowels will go. They will be made the width of the box.

- Before the next phase, we must write our poem and party invitation on the cash register tape. Make your poem and party info use the entire length of the tape. The poem should read something like: "Mom. If roses are red and violets are blue/And one Mother Hubbard lived in a shoe/Then we set this day in honor of you/The one who loved us and raised us and made us cuckoo." Then give the party info.
- Attach each end of the cash register tape to the dowels, but they must pass through the slits first (fig. 2). This can be tricky, but have patience.
- Once the paper is through the slits, take a small piece of Scotch tape and wriggle your fingers into the box to attach. The dowel in the flip lid will be a bit easier.
- After the paper is attached, close the box and tape it shut.
- Now turn the right dowel clockwise so that you start to roll the poem around the dowel.
- When the paper has been completely wound, you're ready to mail it off. All your invitees have to do is wind the left side in a counterclockwise manner and their invitatation will unroll before their eyes (fig. 3).

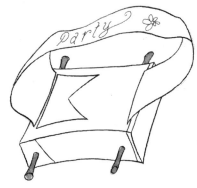

Fig. 2

Fig. 3

crafts

Idle hands are the devil's playground or something like that. But the gist is rather profound: Do something or your liable to go nuts thinking about your problems. Well, after a day spent with dear ol' Mom, your guests might be rather appreciative if you have some group crafts ready to keep their hands busy. Let's make some trivets and a plant hanger. They are two very useful items that you can present to Mom the next time you see her.

Sanitorium-Style Popsicle Stick Trivets

YOU'LL NEED
104 Popsicle sticks (If you're not a Popsicle fanatic and can't save a bunch, most craft stores sell plain Popsicle sticks)
Elmer's glue
Poster paints
Paintbrushes

- For each trivet you'll need 13 popsicle sticks.
- Place 2 of them on your work area 4" apart. These will be the base.
- The rest of the sticks will be laid over these perpendicularly. Before you do this, however, slather some Elmer's onto the base sticks. The top sticks should be arranged side by side, with no space between them.

- Let them dry.
- Once dry, it's time to paint. Paint on images of the day or paint each Popsicle stick a different color for a striped effect. Each person's individuality should be encouraged.

Macramé Plant Hangers

FOR EACH HANGER YOU'LL NEED Twenty-four yards of macramé yarn

- Cut the yarn into 6 lengths measuring 4 yards each.
- Fold the lengths at the middle and knot them.
- Take four of the strands and start knotting, using the basic flat knot, which is in effect the square knot. You start by taking the outside strand on the right and laying it over the two middle strands and under the outside one. Then take the outside one under the two middle strands and up through the space between the first strand and the two middle ones. Repeat this step, only inverting it, and there's your first knot.
- Repeat until there is 6" of yarn unknotted at the bottom.
- After you have made three strands of the knots, we're going to make the base.
- Take two strands from one section and two from the one next to it. With these four strands, make a square knot.
- Repeat on the other strands, then pull them together and knot the dangling strands.

Voilà! Your mother will have a new plant hanger.

Physical Therapy Basket Weaving

Something a bit more challenging for the really strung out-guest might be basket weaving. The manipulation of the sturdy, stubborn reeds into a thing of beauty can bring the most introverted out of their funk.

FOR EACH BASKET YOU'LL NEED

Eight pieces of sturdy reed (spokes) 1' long
A bunch of less sturdy reed (weaver)
Penknife

- Begin by soaking all the reeds in water so that they are more pliable. The spokes will remain a bit more dense.
- Separate the spokes into two groups of four.
- Split the center of one group and then insert the other group through the openings. They should be at right angles and look like a cross.
- Begin by looping one end of the weaver around one set of spokes, and then weave clockwise, under four and over four, continuing around three times.
- Change the pattern to over two, under one, continuing around, all the while spreading the spokes farther apart.
- When you get to the point when you have 2" of spoke left at the end, it's time to make the border.
- Bend over each spoke in a loop and insert the end down into the weaving beside the spoke on its right. Continue around until all the spokes have been inserted into the weaving.

games & things

"My Childhood Was Sooo Bad . . ." Telephone Game

Everyone sits in a circle, and one person starts by whispering into the ear of the person to their right, "My childhood was so bad . . ." and tells them a little story (real or made up) about their childhood. For instance, "My childhood was so bad that when my father left my mother, my mother invited the garbageman to come live with us and we had to eat scraps that he got on the job for dinner." The person who listened now turns to the person to their right and repeats what he or she just heard, adding to it a new incident. This continues all the way around the circle, with the last person telling the whole sad story out loud to the rest of the group.

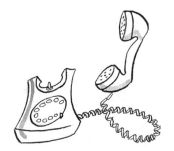

Who Am I?

Everyone gets a small piece of paper and writes the name of a famous mother on it. The mother can be dead or alive, a fictional mother, or the mother of someone at the party. Then everyone sticks the paper onto the forehead of the person sitting on their right and they in essence become that mother. It is now everyone's job to find out who they are by asking yes or no questions such as "Am I a famous entertainer?" or "Was I alive in the nineteenth century?" to the person on their right. This is done in a round robin fashion and anyone can start. Every time the response is yes, that person may ask another question, but if the response is no, the questioning moves on to the next person. The first person to guess who she is wins.

Ketchup Rorschach Tests

Take a piece of paper and fold it in half. Now open it and pour a small blob of ketchup near the center of the paper. Fold it again, then open it, and have each guest say what it looks like to them. The group can then analyze each answer.

Millie Jackson
Feelin Bitchy
Spring Records, 1977
"You Created a Monster"

Peggy Lee
Is That All There Is?
Capitol Records

Alan Sherman
My Son The Nut
Warner Bros., 1963
"Hello Muddah, Hello Fadduh!"

Tom Petty and The Heartbreakers
Damn the Torpedos
MCA Records, 1979
"Refugee"

Charlene
"I've Never Been to Me"
Motown, 1976
45 rpm

The Joey Heatherton Album
MGM Records, 1972
"Crazy"

Doris Day's Greatest Hits
Columbia Records
"Whatever Will Be, Will Be (Que Sera, Sera)"

Carly Simon
The Best of Carly Simon
Elektra, 1975
"Haven't Got Time for the Pain"

Claudine Longet
The Look of Love
A&M Records

Valley of the Dolls
Sound Track
20th Century Fox Records, 1967
"I'll Plant My Own Tree"

Van McCoy
Disco Baby
Avco Records, 1975
"Turn This Mother Out"

Buona Sera, Mrs. Campbell
Sound Track
United Artists Records, Inc., 1969
"A Blessed Event"

cocktails

Mother's Milk White Russians Served in Baby Bottles

Since this party takes place after an encounter with Momma on her day, we might all feel a bit infantile, spent, in need of a beverage that gave us comfort at those tender ages before life became so complicated. But wait, let's not get carried away. I'm sure no one has a supply of formula or mother's milk in the fridge. Instead, let's drink something that's both sweet and creamy and with enough kick to get us through the rest of the evening. Let's drink White Russians.

Just because we've decided to have an adult drink that only has the faintest resemblance to our favorite formula (the milk, right?) that doesn't mean that it can't look like our favorite formula. So let's serve our White Russians in baby bottles.

YOU'LL NEED

Ice
Two bottles of Kahlúa
Two bottles of vodka
Two quarts of milk
Twelve baby bottles with nipple caps

Fill each bottle with ice. Then pour in equal amounts of the Kahlúa, vodka, and milk. Attach the nipples and shake—No, not you!—the bottles. Then suckle to your heart's content.

Miss Party Fabulous Says: Goo goo ga ga, baby.

recipes

**Compose
Yourself
Asparagus and
Shrimp Soup**

2½ lb. asparagus
1 bunch spinach
2 Idaho potatoes
1½ lb. tiger shrimp

4 qt. chicken stock
 (see recipe on page 21)
2 oz. olive oil
2 oz. brandy
Salt and pepper

Clean asparagus, cut off tips, and set tips aside for garnish. Cut asparagus stems into large pieces; set aside.

Wash spinach, spin dry, and set aside.

Peel, rinse, and dice potatoes. Set aside. Peel and devein shrimp. Be sure to save the shells.

In a stockpot, bring chicken stock to a boil.

While the stock is heating up, heat olive oil in a sauté pan. Sauté shrimp shells for 1 minute and deglaze with brandy. (Hold the pan at arm's length, since the brandy may flame.)

Add shells and any liquid from the sauté pan to boiling stock. Reduce heat and simmer for 45 minutes. With a slotted spoon, remove shells and discard. Next, add the shrimp and asparagus tips to stock. Simmer for 3 minutes with a slotted spoon, remove shrimp and asparagus tips, let cool, cover, and refrigerate.

Add potatoes and asparagus pieces to stock. Simmer for an additional 30 to 40 minutes or until vegetables are soft. Add spinach.

Puree soup with a stick blender, strain soup through a sieve, and season with salt and pepper.

Ladle soup into warm bowls and garnish with shrimp and asparagus tips.

Chicken Club Sandwiches

1 cup canola oil
2 tablespoons garlic, chopped
Salt and pepper
8 5-oz. chicken cutlets
1 cup mayonnaise
1 tablespoon cayenne

1 tablespoon grated orange zest
8 onion rolls
8 leaves romaine
8 slices tomato
16 strips smoked bacon, cooked

THE MARINADE Mix oil, garlic, and a pinch of salt and pepper. In a shallow pan, cover the chicken cutlets with the marinade. Cover and refrigerate overnight.

THE ASSEMBLY Preheat oven to 350°. In a bowl, mix the mayonnaise, cayenne, and orange zest. Set aside.

In a large sauté pan, cook the cutlets for 3 minutes on each side. Transfer to a shallow pan and finish in oven for 2 minutes.

Split rolls and toast in oven for 1 minute. Brush each side of roll with orange-cayenne mayonnaise. Place chicken breast on roll and top with 1 leaf of romaine, 1 slice of tomato, and 2 strips of bacon.

Miss Party Fabulous Says: If it's a nice night and you've got the grill all set up, head outdoors and cook in the moonlight.

Pure Contentment Almond-Sour Cream Cheesecake

2 cups almond slices, toasted
1¼ cups graham cracker crumbs
1¼ cups sugar
¼ cup unsalted butter, melted
1¼ lb. cream cheese
4 tablespoons heavy cream

2 eggs
1 egg yolk
2 teaspoons vanilla extract
10 oz. sour cream
7 tablespoons confectioners' sugar
1 tablespoon cinnamon

Preheat oven to 325°.

To toast almond slices, sprinkle on cookie sheet and place in oven for 4 minutes.

In a food processor, mix the graham cracker crumbs, ¼ cup sugar, and the melted butter. Press this mixture into the bottom of a 9" springform pan.

Using a kitchen aid with a paddle attachment, beat cream cheese until smooth. Add the remaining sugar, heavy cream, eggs, egg yolk, and vanilla. Beat for 5 to 7 minutes. Fill pan with mixture. Bake for 1¼ hours. If top of cake begins to brown too quickly, cover loosely with aluminum foil. Pierce cake in center with a toothpick. If it comes out clean, the cake is done.

Mix sour cream and confectioners' sugar. When cake is cool, spread this over top of cheesecake. Garnish cake with toasted almond slices and cinnamon.

Place cake in refrigerator overnight. Run a knife around edge of cake before releasing spring on pan.

Sugar-Rush Chocolate-Pistachio Clusters

8 oz. Calabaut chocolate, semisweet
⅔ cup condensed sweetened milk
¾ cup pistachio nuts, chopped

In a double boiler, melt chocolate until smooth (about 7 to 8 minutes). Be careful not to let water boil in the double boiler. Remove chocolate from heat. Mix in the condensed milk and pistachios.

Cover a sheet tray with wax paper and, using a tablespoon, spoon clusters onto tray.

Refrigerate for at least 45 minutes before serving.

Lemon/Orange/ Poppy Seed Cookies

1 cup sugar
½ cup unsalted butter, soft
Pinch of salt
1 teaspoon vanilla
2 eggs
½ cup milk

1 teaspoon grated lemon zest
1 teaspoon grated orange zest
2 cups all-purpose flour
2 teaspoons baking soda
½ cup poppy seeds

Preheat oven to 350°.

In a medium bowl, cream together the sugar, butter, salt, and vanilla until fluffy. Mix in eggs, milk, and zest. Fold in flour and baking soda.

Wrap dough in plastic wrap and refrigerate for one hour. On a lightly floured cutting board, roll out dough ½" thick. With a round cookie cutter, cut out cookies. Place cookies 1" apart on a lightly greased cookie sheet. Sprinkle each with a pinch of poppy seeds and bake on center rack of oven for 10 minutes or until golden brown.

Remove, let cool, and arrange on platter.

Queens in White Satin
(A Drag Prom for Thirty-five)

MENU

Dreamgirl Mushroom Ceviche
Thai Beef Salad
Diva Smoked Chicken Citrus Salad
Figure-Saving Orzo Salad
Encore! Chocolate Brownies

**GAMES AND
THINGS**

Touch-Up, Dress-Up
Let's Play Prom Photos
The Performances

COCKTAILS

Girly-Girl Sidecars

CRAFTS

Panty Hose Invitations
Photo-Op Background
Party Fabulous Special Memory Frames
Wig Hats

Parties are just little experiments in living. A party is an opportunity to be who you want to be and to create the world you want to live in. Sometimes, be you a man or a woman, that means delving into your other side—exploring your yin or your yang.

This party is like a prom for all of you who never got to go to one in high school or for those of you who went but secretly wanted to trade your tux for a slinky dress. This time, you get to do it your way.

Drag is an expensive, time-consuming business. The cost of panty hose alone—and the pros sometimes wear as many as three pairs at the same time—is enough to deplete your piggy bank. There are a million details to attend to like getting the padding just right, getting used to your heels, remembering to plunge your face into a bowl of ice to ward off that 10 o'clock shadow. It can get to be too much, and that's why we stick to a more low-key kind of drag. We appreciate perfection in others but don't necessarily strive for it ourselves. It's better not to have too many expectations, because it's rare that things turn out right. For instance, you may be thinking Liz Taylor, but all your friends are stunned by your amazing likeness to Shelly Winters.

Special Moments

There are many ways around this. One is to allow your drag persona to evolve by starting off slow: just a wig and some earrings perhaps, worn with your usual, everyday jeans and a shirt. Later on, you might want to add a boa, maybe some pumps.

Todd does a special kind of pan-sexual, postmodern drag. He only dresses up in outfits made out of old Twister boards. He does full makeup and outrageous wigs, but no padding. And when it comes to lip-synching, he doesn't restrict himself; he might do anything from Petula Clark to the Doors. He isn't male, he isn't female, he's just *other*.

There are two things that have to happen before the performances start. One is, you have to eat. That's because you'll need something in your stomach so you can get really lit, which is the second imperative. You have to be pretty toasted before you can give your performance its all, you know? As host/ess, you'll want to set up a makeshift stage. It can be as simple or as elaborate as you want it to be, anything from a clearing at one end of your living room to a little platform and curtain type thing. You might want to have a stool on hand for those who do the slower ballads. During the performances, crank the music up loud—it's a necessity of drag. Don't forget to have your little dress-up area, with extra wigs, dresses, and jewelry for those who were too reluctant to come in drag but somehow get swept up in the enthusiasm during the course of the party and want to indulge themselves. Also, go to the Salvation Army and pick up a dozen or so of those old polyester tuxedo jackets from the '70s, and make anyone who's not in drag wear them—they are the escorts for the evening.

If you follow these guidelines, we promise you that this post–high school, postmodern prom can be every bit as special as your high school prom was—and maybe even more so. By the end of the last number, you'll have couples slow dancing and making out in the shadows. And then you'll smile to yourself, and you'll know to never underestimate the power of these three key prom-night elements: love, laughter, and a couple of wigs.

Miss Party Fabulous's Advice for the Ladies: All you real girls out there can come in boy drag (then you're called a drag king) or you can do girl drag—dress up as a mega-girl! After all, the type of women men dress up as have nothing to do with real women, whatsoever.

Panty Hose Invitations

Oh Beelzebub! How many times have you had to show up in drag, and at the last minute, when you're already forty-five minutes late, you put on your panty hose and there's one humungous run! Who can count? And are you prepared the next time? No! Because you're thinking about your dress or the song that you're going to perform that night, realizing you only know half the words. So, to remedy this gut-wrenching situation for all your guests on Drag Prom Night, you're going to send them an extra pair of panty hose as their invitation. Size doesn't matter because you're only going to buy queen size. You're also only going to get them the cheapest sheers, so let's hope everyone has buzzed their legs.

YOU'LL NEED

Three sheets of 12" × 18" white construction paper
Scissors
Red and black felt-tip pens
Thirty-five pairs of cheap pantyhose
Thirty-five 12" × 18" Manila envelopes

- Cut each piece of construction paper into 12 rectangles measuring 3" × 4".
- We are going to create four different images: a high-heel shoe, a lipstick, a wig, and lips. One image per rectangle.
- Since we have thirty-five invitations to write out, we will make nine copies of each image.

- Very few of us are real artists, so take the images that we are giving you and make patterns that you can use for your images.
- Cut them out and write all the pertinent party info on them.
- Stuff them into the panty hose, then stuff the pantyhose into the Manila envelopes, label, and mail.

Your responsibility to the other girls is over. Concentrate on your fierce dress (and the trellis).

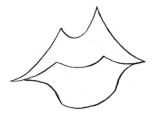

Photo-Op Background

Every prom must have its little area set aside for the photo ops. At Todd's, there was a little pool lined in green plastic and edged in bricks with a fountain that shot a stream of water like an overzealous drinking fountain. To the side was a pedestal with an arrangement of red and white carnations (our school colors) and there was a drape of some kind of fabric coming down in back. It was very classy. And this prom is no exception.

YOU'LL NEED

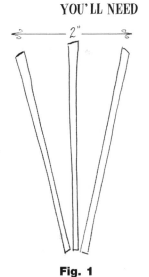

Fig. 1

Wood:
> Three ⅝" lattices, 7' long
> One ⅝" lattice, 2' long
> One ⅝" lattice, 1½' long
> One ⅝" lattice, 1' long

Hardware:
> Staple gun
> White spray paint
> Ten yards of white satin
> Paper flowers
> Plastic ivy
> Stapler

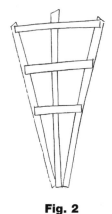

Fig. 2

- Lay out the 7' pieces of lattice on the floor in a fan shape (fig. 1). The bottoms will meet but not overlap, and the two outside pieces will be 2' apart at the top with the center piece going straight up the middle.

- Lay the three other pieces of lattice over these in a crisscross manner (fig. 2). The 2' piece across the top, the 1½' piece in the middle, and the 1' piece toward the bottom.
- Staple gun at all the points where the lattice overlaps. Use ¼" staples so that the staples won't protrude to the other side.
- Flip it over and spray-paint it white.
- When the paint has dried, attach it to the wall of the photo-op area either with the staple gun (using longer staples than before) or with nails.
- Now take the fabric and tie it in a knot at the middle.
- Attach the knot to the wall just above the middle lattice.
- Then tack the fabric once more to the wall 1½' from the knot on either side.
- Bring the fabric that is on the floor around to the front to form a little round area of fabric, and this will be where your guests will stand.
- Now decorate the trellis with paper flowers and plastic ivy. Staple a few of the larger flowers over the knot and some of the smaller ones onto the fabric. The prom guest should be engulfed in flowers.

Party Fabulous Special Memory Frames

If you're going to be taking pictures of someone's very special evening, then you'll need to make sure that they *really* remember how special it was by giving the guests their prom pictures in a lovely Party Fabulous frame. We know that this means you're going to have to churn out over thirty of these babies, but start a few weeks in advance, and just do a couple of stages a night. The process moves faster if it's like an assembly line.

YOU'LL NEED
Eighteen sheets of 12" × 18" lightweight poster board (6 white, 12 assorted colors)
Scissors
Penknife (optional)
Elmer's glue
Silver glitter
Glue stick

- First thing to do is take all the assorted-colored poster board sheets and cut them up. Cut each board into three pieces measuring 12" × 6".
- Fold each piece to make a 6" × 6" square.
- Cut out a 3" square from the center of the right-hand page. Since the page is a 6" square, just measure 1½" around (the crease has become an edge).
- Or on a piece of scrap paper cut out a 3" square to use as an outline and center it on the page using 1½" borders. Trace the square and then cut it out. This is where I would use a penknife to make very clean lines but the scissors will do.

- Now you have the base frame.
- To decorate the frame page, take your Elmer's glue and squirt it around the border in some stunning design.
- Sprinkle on the glitter. Remove the excess and let dry.

- Or if you don't want a design per se, you can smear the glue all over the picture border, then glitter it up, and you've got a totally glittery frame. The design is up to you.

- Now it's time to cut up the white poster board. Cut one board into 6 pieces measuring 6" × 6" so you'll get six squares per board. These will be used as the backing for the Polaroids.
- The final stage of the frames comes after the Polaroids have been taken.
- After the Polaroid has been taken, give the bottom white border of the Polaroid a swipe of the glue stick.
  - Center the actual photo (which measures 3" × 3", just like the opening we made) with the frame opening.
  - Give the bottom juncture, where we applied some glue stick, a little pressure.
  - Apply the glue stick around the periphery of the backing, then attach to the back side of the frame. This will keep the photo in place and our georgeous prom memory is done.

Miss Party Fabulous Says: Plant a big kiss on the front of each photo frame to give that extra special personal touch.

Wig Hats

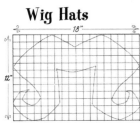

Fig. 1

This crown is an all-time crowd pleaser. Real wigs can make people feel a bit self-conscious, heaven knows why. But a lovely, two-dimensional wig hat perks them right up. They feel zany, even wacky. They're doin' drag, but not really. We've included this crown for the drag prom night because there will always be those Party Fabulous guests that either didn't get to the wig shop on time or they weren't able to come up with the coins for a wig (let me tell you, they can cost a bundle). These are your reserve so no one will be left wigless.

YOU'LL NEED

12" × 18" construction paper in an assortment of hair-tone colors, plus some blues or greens for the bows
Scissors
Stapler
Tape

Fig. 2

- First thing you need to do is make a construction paper headband. Use your own head as a guide.
- Take one piece of paper and fold it lengthwise in thirds. Cut along the creases.
- Take one of the three strips and fold it in half. Cut along the crease.
- Staple a long piece and a short piece together, then wrap the whole thing around your head and staple the ends together to fit.
- Now we need to make the wig part. On a piece of construction paper, outline the shape of your wig (fig. 1). Cut it out.
- Now, cut out a bow from the pastel paper.
- Staple your wig to the headband, being careful to staple close to the center. Then tape on the bow so that it covers the staple (fig. 2).

Miss Party Fabulous Says: As with any hairstyle, a ribbon or barette or flower give each wig that extra added zip.

games & things

At this party, you'll have your dress-up area set up for the last-minute drag queens, and your photo-op area where one guest can play photographer and take Polaroids of the happy couples. But the main activity is the drag performance, of course! Could you want anything more, girlfriend? The most helpful hints we can give when it comes to performing is make every gesture as big as possible, give a lot of thought to choosing your material, and spend a lot of time practicing in front of the mirror.

You'll find some song suggestions in the music section, and what follows are some of the stock movements for the drag queen repertoire:

welcome T

closing X

quivering lower lip

① *reach*
② *pick*
③ *grab*

cherry picking

the Point

never this...

...always this!

Hairspray
Sound Track
MCA Records

A Golden Encore
Hit Tunes That Sold Over a Million
Columbia Records
"I Feel Pretty" (Julie Andrews)

Dream Girls
Sound Track
Geffen Records, 1982

Aerosmith
"Dude (Looks Like a Lady)"
Geffen Records, 1987
45 rpm

Julie Brown
I Like 'Em Big and Stupid
Stymie Music, Inc., 1982
"Homecoming Queen's Got a Gun"

Shirley Bassey's Greatest Hits
United Artists Records, 1975
"Goldfinger"

Diana Ross and the Supremes
Sing and Perform Funny Girl
Motown Records, 1968

The Adventures of Priscilla
Queen of The Desert
Polydor Records Australia, 1994

Angela Lansbury as Mame
Sound Track
Columbia Records
"Bosom Buddies"

Barbra Striesand and
Kris Kristofferson
A Star Is Born Sound Track
Warner Bros. Records, 1976
"Queen Bee"

Madonna
You Can Dance
Sire Records Co., 1987
"Holiday"

Gladys Knight and The Pips
Touch
Columbia Records, 1981
"I Will Survive"

cocktails

Girly-Girl Sidecars

Drag queens! What the hell do you serve them? Beer? Out of the question! Vodka stingers? Nahh, the name's good, but who really drinks crème de menthe any more? And nothing with gin, that's for sure. These girls are crazy enough, you don't need to send them into the stratosphere by giving them gin. What you need is something a little girlie, a little retro. Something like sidecars! That sounds perfect. Definitely girlie, positively retro, and tasty, too. We'll even sugar the rims because these girls need all the extra sweetness they can get.

YOU'LL NEED

Brandy
Rose's Lime Juice
Triple Sec
Grapefruit juice
Sugar
Orange slices

It's pitcher time again, so let's get them out of the closet.

A sidecar is basically a margarita with brandy, so if you have a good margarita recipe, there's no need to read on, just substitute brandy for tequila. For you others, fill a pitcher with ice. Pour in ½ bottle of brandy, 8 oz. of Rose's, 16 oz. of Triple Sec, and a healthy splash of grapefruit juice. Stir it up. Then strain into a martini glass (actually there is such a thing as a sidecar

glass, but who knows what it looks like) where the rim has been dusted with sugar. Garnish with an orange slice.

Miss Party Fabulous Says: Even with the sugar rim, you better serve these with a straw. Drag queens don't like to muss their lipstick.

recipes

Dreamgirl Mushroom Ceviche

10 lb. wild mushrooms (combine oyster, crimini, chanterelle, and white trumpet)
1 bunch tarragon
1 bunch cilantro
1 cup poblano chilies, diced, seeded
1 cup red onion, diced
2 cups lime juice
1 cup extra-virgin olive oil
Salt and pepper
1 head Bibb lettuce
1 head radicchio
Toast points

Thoroughly wash mushrooms and remove stems. Leave mushrooms whole unless unusually large.

Chop the tarragon and cilantro, but leave a few sprigs of each for garnish.

Combine all ingredients except Bibb lettuce, radicchio, and toast points in a large bowl. Season with salt and pepper. Wrap and refrigerate overnight.

When ready to serve, bring up to room temperature and garnish a large platter with the Bibb lettuce and radicchio. Spoon mushrooms onto platter and garnish with sprigs of herbs.

Serve a basket of toast points on the side.

Thai Beef Salad

THE MARINADE

Juice of 12 limes	10 shallots, minced
2 cups rice vinegar	10 cloves garlic, minced
4 cups fish sauce	1 bunch cilantro, chopped
1 cup soy sauce	9 lb. beef tenderloin (de-fatted)
10 Thai chilies, split	

In a bowl, mix all ingredients except the tenderloin. Place the tenderloin in a shallow pan and pour marinade over the top. Cover and refrigerate overnight. Remember to turn beef occasionally to marinate completely.

THE ASSEMBLY

6 carrots, julienned	Salad dressing
2 chayote, julienned	1 bunch mint
3 red peppers, julienned	1 bunch cilantro
1 cup unsalted peanuts, chopped	

Preheat oven to 450°.

First you need to sear the tenderloin. Heat a large sauté pan and brown beef on all sides (about 5 minutes). Place tenderloin on rack in roasting pan and roast for 10 to 12 minutes. Set aside and let cool. Slice tenderloin in half lengthwise, then slice very thin against the grain.

In a large bowl, mix the vegetables, peanuts, and beef. Toss with the dressing. Arrange salad on a large platter and garnish with sprigs of mint and cilantro.

THE DRESSING

1 cup lime juice	2 oz. honey
1 cup fish sauce	2 oz. sesame oil

Whisk together; toss with salad.

Diva Smoked Chicken Citrus Salad

1 cup pumpkin seeds, toasted
8 lb. smoked boneless chicken breast
2 pineapples, peeled, diced
2 red onions, minced
3 jalapeños, seeded, julienned
2 cups red grapes, halved

1 cup olive oil
Juice of 3 limes
1 bunch tarragon, chopped
Salt and pepper
1 orange

Preheat oven to 350°.

To toast the pumpkin seeds, place on a sheet tray and toast in the oven for 10 minutes. Chop the pumpkin seeds. Set aside.

In a large bowl, combine all ingredients except orange; cover and refrigerate.

Should be prepared at least 2 hours before party.

When ready to serve, transfer to a large platter and garnish with twisted slices of orange.

Figure-Saving Orzo Salad

3 lb. orzo
5 red peppers
4 oz. canola oil
1 bunch basil

2 cups olive oil
4 oz. rice vinegar
Salt and pepper

Preheat oven to 500°.

Cook orzo as per directions on package. Set aside.

Next we need to roast and puree the red peppers. Preheat oven to 500°. Rub each pepper with canola oil. Place peppers on rack in oven above cookie sheet. Roast for 20 to 25 minutes. Remove from oven and immerse peppers in a pan of ice water. When peppers are cool, rinse skin off under running water. Remove seeds and puree in a food processor. Set aside.

Julienne most of the basil leaves, but save some for garnish.

In a large bowl combine all ingredients.

Transfer to a large platter and garnish with basil leaves.

Encore! Chocolate Brownies

1 lb. 2 oz. Calabaut chocolate, semisweet
2 lb. 2 oz. butter
6 cups sugar
18 eggs
2 tablespoons vanilla extract

3 cups all-purpose flour
1 tablespoon plus 1 teaspoon baking powder
¾ teaspoon salt
1½ cups walnuts, chopped
1½ cups chocolate chips, semisweet

Preheat oven to 350°.

Chop chocolate into small chunks. In a double boiler, combine Calabaut chocolate and butter and melt until smooth (about 10–12 minutes). Remove from heat and let cool for a few minutes. Transfer chocolate to a large bowl, whisk in sugar, and then add eggs one at a time, beating continuously. Add vanilla. Add flour, baking powder, salt, 1 cup walnuts, and 1 cup chocolate chips, and fold into chocolate mixture. Line 2 baking trays with baking paper. Grease paper and sides of pans. Pour batter evenly into pans.

Sprinkle remaining chocolate chips and walnuts evenly on top of batter. Bake for 25 minutes.

Allow to cool while still in pans, then slice into 2" squares. Be sure to remove baking paper from bottom of brownies!

Arrange on large platter.

Comin' Out Cookout
(A Casual Ritual for Twenty-five)

MENU Barbecued Ribs and Shrimp
Trout Grilled in Foil
Lamb and Vegetable Kabobs with Cucumber-Mint Salsa and
    Lemon-Caper Aioli
Grilled Corn on the Cob
Corn Bread
Focaccia Salad
Potato Salad
Strawberry Shortcake

GAMES AND Group Totem
THINGS Group Poem
Essence
Human Maypole
Sardines

COCKTAILS Essential Freedom Elixir

CRAFTS Closet Invitations
 Daisy-Chain Head Wreaths

If coming out meant nothing more than putting on a jacket and locking the door behind you, there'd be no reason to celebrate it with a cookout. Unfortunately, coming out can more accurately be described as a process of burrowing through a tunnel filled with cobwebs of anxiety, guilt, frustration and anger. But after you make it through the shadows and re-emerge into a brand-new light, it's time to shout it out from the highest mountain and have a barbeque!

It's a mad, mad, mad world made even madder when someone comes on out. Your parents may blame themselves, but we say they should take the credit! Some doors may slam, but who needs to be in when you'd rather be out! Seriously, though, it all takes loads of courage and oftentimes you'll feel like it's just you against the world.

Coming out doesn't all happen in one grand moment. It is preceded by years of *knowing*, without really knowing. It's an accumulation of little moments, like the realization that you have the most unerring sense of style of any of the little boys in your 6th grade class, or, for a little girl, the decision to take shop class instead of home ec. After years of little peculiarities, you finally wake up one morning and think, 'Gosh, I'm gay!', and then another part of you thinks, 'Of course you are, silly!'

When a friend of yours is struggling with this new rite of passage, help him or her out by throwing this Comin' Out Cookout. It's an indoctrination for people who don't really want a private moment to contemplate it all. It should have a ritualistic, almost tribal aspect. We all started our rituals together without even knowing it. That's why we think it's so important for friends to come together at this time to show support for the one who's coming out and to celebrate this momentous occasion in his or her life. It's a little like a bar mitzvah, kind of like a debutante ball. But in our declasse world, it's just a comin' out cookout.

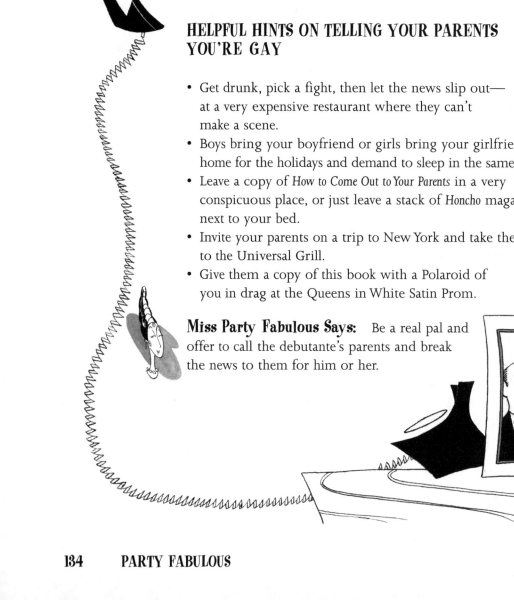

HELPFUL HINTS ON TELLING YOUR PARENTS YOU'RE GAY

- Get drunk, pick a fight, then let the news slip out—
  at a very expensive restaurant where they can't
  make a scene.
- Boys bring your boyfriend or girls bring your girlfriend
  home for the holidays and demand to sleep in the same room.
- Leave a copy of *How to Come Out to Your Parents* in a very
  conspicuous place, or just leave a stack of *Honcho* magazines
  next to your bed.
- Invite your parents on a trip to New York and take them
  to the Universal Grill.
- Give them a copy of this book with a Polaroid of
  you in drag at the Queens in White Satin Prom.

Miss Party Fabulous Says: Be a real pal and
offer to call the debutante's parents and break
the news to them for him or her.

Closet Invitations

This is such a special occasion that we want our guests to know it as soon as they get their invitations in the mail. They need to understand and feel the essence of the party that they will be attending. Someone is taking a big step in his or her life. This person's sense of self and view of life will be forever changed. He or she is coming out of the closet!

YOU'LL NEED

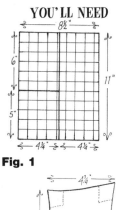

Fig. 1

Thirteen pieces of lightweight brown 8½" × 11" poster board
Scotch tape
Black felt-tip pen
Lavender tissue paper
Twenty-five dolls (female or male depending on the honoree, also cheap, cheap, cheap. I found some that were 69 cents and 4" tall)

- Okay, let's make our closet. Oh right, forgot to tell you: the invitation is going to literally be the honoree coming out of a closet.
- Let's begin. Take one piece of the poster board and cut it lengthwise so that you end up with two 4¼" × 11" pieces (fig. 1). Set one aside for the next closet.
- Then cut this piece so that you end up with two different-sized pieces: one 4¼" × 6" and the other 4¼" × 5" (fig. 1).
- With the larger of the two pieces, trace a 1" × 1" square in each of the corners. Cut them out (fig. 2).

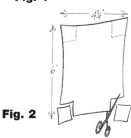

Fig. 2

Fig. 3

Fig. 4

- Now fold each side into the center, forming a crease between the corners of the four cut-out squares. Once the crease has been formed, let each side stand perpendicular to the bottom and tape where each side meets (fig. 3) and there's the closet's base.
- For the door, cut the smaller of the two pieces so that you end up with a piece that is 2½" × 5" (fig. 4).
- Draw on a doorknob and then attach to the base by using two pieces of tape on the inside of the box (the tape will act as hinges for the door) (fig. 5).
- Also on the front of the door it is probably a good idea to write CLOSET over the top.
- Line the box with some tissue paper so the honoree (the doll) won't be jostled while the invitation is being mailed.
- Place the honoree in the box along with a little note giving all the party info. Close the door and lock with a small piece of tape.
- Place the closet in a mailing box lined with newspapers. Again, no jostling.
- Repeat.
- Then it's off to the post office. The postman is going to love you by now.

Fig. 5

Daisy-Chain Head Wreaths

There are not a lot of crafts to do while you're romping through the open air, communing with Mother Nature. Frolicking and dancing with Dionysian abandon. Flowers are everywhere, fresh and fragrant and just waiting to be picked. They will make perfect Party Fabulous crowns.

YOU'LL NEED Freshly picked flowers

- Send everyone off to gather their bunch of flowers. (If your cookout is open air but not quite in nature, i.e., on your terrace or in your backyard, have a big bunch of daisies ready that you bought beforehand.)
- Start with two flowers. Break off the stems about 5" from the flower or where the stem is starting to get more rigid.
- Then tie the bottom of one stem to the other stem at about 2" from the flower. Use a square knot, kneading the stems as you tie so as to make them more pliable.
- Continue on, one flower at a time, knotting the bottom of the new stem to just below the flower of the last until you have made a garland that can fit around your head.

Oh Ophelia! You look just gorgeous.

games & things

There's just so much to do at this party. Where to begin?

Group Totem

A totem is an object that serves as a symbol or emblem for a tribe. The totems can be anything from a necklace to a sculpture. The comer-outer can even make one himself, as a symbol of exactly where he is at this moment. This is another group activity where you'll provide some materials—in this case, maybe some photos of the comer-outer, some old magazines, small plastic figurines, paints, glue, twine, leather thongs, beads—and then you set your guests out on their own. Let them search the woods for rocks, feathers, branches, flowers, and old bones with which to create. When everyone is finished, gather all the totems together, creating an altar. Decorate with candles.

Before the comer-outer arrives, gather up your guests and coauthor a poem honoring him or her. It might go something like this:

Group Poem

This is a time to dance and play,
For freedom is soon on the way,
Because this is the special day,
When Peter tells the world he's gay.
We've waited for this day so long,
We knew that we could not be wrong,
When, behind his back, we'd say,
"Don't tell me that he's not gay."

Make it a little longer, a little more personal. Toss in all those little secrets you know about the comer-outer. Then tuck it away for later on in the festivities.

Essence

One person leaves the group. The rest of the group decides who is it (the it person can be either someone who is present or the person who left the room). When the person who has left the room comes back, he tries to determine who is it by asking questions about the essence of the person. For instance, he would ask, "If this person were a tree, what kind of a tree would he be?" or "Is this person a little bit country or a little bit rock 'n' roll?" After having asked every player one question, he makes a guess as to who is it.

Human Maypole

Okay, if you haven't gotten the idea yet, we're creating a little tribal thing here. In advance, make a wreath crown for the comer-outer, using the instructions for the foil wreath in the polenta party chapter. Take twelve lengths of brightly colored ribbon, approximately 3" wide and 12' long, and tie them to the wreath, then cover the wreath with fresh flowers attached with hat pins—just make sure none of them stick out—you don't want it to be a crown of thorns! Now you've got your totems on the altar, and you've got your poem. Place the crown on the head of the comer-outer, and have each guest grab one of the ribbons (there are more guests than ribbons, so have the extra guests toss flower petals and do an interpretative dance). Play "I'm Coming Out" or "I Am What I Am" or whatever you deem appropriate, and start wrapping the ribbons around the comer-outer, in a frolicsome, gay manner. When he/she is all wrapped up in ribbon, turn down the music and read the poem, either in unison or with each guest reading a line. Then unwrap the comer-outer, walk him/her over to the altar, and say, "We now pronounce you *gay!*" Disco dance for awhile, then eat. Got it?

Sardines

Sardines is like hide-and-go-seek, but in reverse. One person hides and everybody else sets off on their own to find him. When someone finds him, they hide with him, until everyone is hiding together. The last person to find them is it, and is the one to hide in the next round.

The Sound of Music
Sound Track
RCA Victor, 1965
"Maria" and "Climb Ev'ry Mountain"

The Best of the Staple Singers
Stax Records
"I'll Take You There" and "Respect Yourself"

The B-52's
Cosmic Thing
Reprise Records, 1989
"Roam" and "Love Shack"

Olivia's Greatest Hits
Volume 2
MCA Records, 1980
"You're the One That I Want"

Sammy Davis, Jr.
I Gotta Be Me
Reprise Records
"If My Friends Could See Me Now"

Barry Manilow
Greatest Hits
Arista Records, 1978
"It's a Miracle"

Harpers Bizarre
Feelin Groovy
Warner Bros
"59th Street Bridge Song"

The Best of Peter, Paul and Mary
Ten Years Together
Warner Bros., 1970
"Puff (The Magic Dragon)"

Lulu Sings **"To Sir with Love"**
Epic Records

The Partridge Family
Up to Date
Bell Records
"I Think I Love You"

Glen Campbell
Gentle on My Mind
Capitol Records
"Mary in the Morning"

Johnny Nash
I Can See Clearly Now
Epic Records
"Stir It Up"

Nat King Cole
Unforgettable
The Longines
Symphonette Society
"Those Lazy Hazy Crazy Days of Summer"

cocktails

Essential Freedom Elixir

When that beautiful summer breeze is blowing and you're frolicking around the maypole, you need something to drink that's as fresh as a summer day: pink lemonade (with vodka of course) and a sprig of freshly picked mint. Mmmmmm!

YOU'LL NEED

2 cups freshly squeezed lemon juice
2 cups sugar
5 gallons water
Grenadine (for color)
Vodka
Mint sprigs

In a 5-gallon thermos, mix the lemon juice, sugar, and water. Stir until the sugar has become dissolved. Add $\frac{1}{8}$ cup of grenadine. In a highball glass filled with ice, pour in one shot of vodka. then fill with the lemonade. Plop in a sprig of mint as a garnish.

recipes

Barbecued Ribs and Shrimp

If you don't want to do one huge comin' out spread, offer up these delicious nibbly bits as a casual starter. This will also free up some room on the grill later on, although as it is, you may have to rent a big-boy-deluxe grill from your local party rental.

THE RIBS

10 lb. pork ribs	1 tablespoon thyme, dry
½ gal. Worcestershire sauce	1 tablespoon rosemary, dry
1 cup garlic powder	1 tablespoon oregano, dry
1 cup paprika	1 tablespoon black pepper
½ cup cayenne pepper	

You will need to marinate the ribs for 24 hours before grilling. Place the rack of ribs in a large pan and rub with the Worcestershire sauce. Combine all other ingredients and rub this onto ribs. Cover and refrigerate overnight.

Barbecue the ribs over a low fire for 45 minutes, turning frequently and basting with the leftover marinade.

THE SHRIMP

5 lb. shrimp (16–20 count)	Salt and pepper
1 cup olive oil	Barbecue sauce

Secure 4 or 5 shrimp per skewer. Brush each side with olive oil and season with salt and pepper. Grill for 2 minutes on one side, turn and brush grilled side with barbecue sauce. Repeat for other side.

BARBECUE SAUCE

1 cup onions, sliced
1 tablespoon bacon fat
1 cup coffee, brewed
1 cup Worcestershire sauce
1 cup ketchup
½ cup honey

½ cup soy sauce
3 cinnamon sticks
1 bay leaf
1 tablespoon ground chipotle chili
1 tablespoon Hoisin sauce

In a medium saucepan, sauté onions in bacon fat until lightly browned, about 5 to 7 minutes. Add all other ingredients and simmer for 2 hours. Strain through a sieve.

Makes about 1 quart.

Trout Grilled in Foil

While at the fish market, you may prefer to have the head and tail removed from your trout. Don't forget to get a large roll of aluminum foil.

10 12-oz. whole trout, boned
10 sprigs of rosemary
1 lb. unsalted butter
1 teaspoon garlic, chopped

1 teaspoon shallots, chopped
Juice of 2 limes
Salt and pepper

Lay each trout skin side down and opened up on a piece of foil. Make sure the foil is large enough to fold over the fillet. Place one rosemary sprig down backbone of each trout.

In a small saucepan over low heat, melt the butter. Add the garlic, shallots, and lime juice to the butter and bring to a boil, stirring constantly so as not to burn. Ladle 1½ oz. of butter mixture over each fillet.

Season with salt and pepper, fold foil over fillet, and crimp edges to seal the foil. Grill for 10 to 12 minutes.

Miss Party Fabulous Says: You decide: More trout or more lamb? If you want 20 trout, start fishing now, and just double all the other ingredients.

Lamb and Vegetable Kabobs with Cucumber-Mint Salsa and Lemon-Caper Aioli

1 8–10 lb. leg of lamb
1 cup olive oil
2 cups red wine vinegar
2 cups yogurt

2 oz. lemon juice
½ cup garlic, chopped
1 tablespoon rosemary, chopped

When you purchase the lamb from your butcher, have the lamb cleaned and cut into 1" cubes (you might want to bring your butcher a bottle of good champagne or some chocolates).

You will need to marinate the lamb for 24 hours before grilling. In a bowl, combine all ingredients except for the lamb. Place the lamb in a shallow pan and add the marinade, mixing thoroughly. Cover and refrigerate overnight.

THE ASSEMBLY

5 medium red onions
3 baby eggplants
4 medium squash (yellow and green)

5 peppers (combine red, yellow, and green)
Salt and pepper

Cut each onion into 6 wedges, slice eggplant and squash into ½" slices, and julienne the peppers.

When you're ready to grill, put 6 or 7 pieces of lamb on each skewer (12") alternating with a combination of cut vegetables. Season with salt and pepper. Grill for 8 to 10 minutes, turning occasionally.

Miss Party Fabulous Says: Here's a little trick I learned at a party in Halifax. If you're using wooden skewers or thick rosemary stems, soak them for 1 hour in warm water before skewering—they won't burn so badly when grilled.

LEMON-CAPER AIOLI

1 egg	2 tablespoons capers
2 egg yolks	1 tablespoon Dijon mustard
Juice of 1 lemon	10 oz. canola oil
Zest of 3 lemons	2 oz. olive oil
3 cloves garlic, peeled	

In a food processor, puree all ingredients except the canola and olive oils. While still blending, add both oils in a slow, steady stream. Aioli should be thick and smooth. Serve in a festive bowl.

CUCUMBER-MINT SALSA

10 cucumbers, peeled, seeded, diced	3 tablespoons lemon juice
2 red onions, diced	1 tablespoon extra-virgin olive oil
1 clove garlic, diced	1 bunch mint, chopped
1 tablespoon sugar	Salt and pepper

Toss everything together in a large bowl. Season with salt and pepper. Refrigerate for at least 1 hour before serving. Serve in a festive bowl.

Grilled Corn on the Cob

There are many different ways to grill corn on the cob. We've seen it buried in the ground under hot coals, thrown right from the cornfield onto the grill, and one night, just a little tipsy we were, poured right from a can of Del Monte onto a lovely bed of ash. Corn is best when prepared following these simple directions. To save some quality cookout time and get in that extra game of horseshoes, you may want to blanch the corn the day before.

2 doz. ears corn on the cob	½ lb. unsalted butter, melted
½ cup corn oil	Salt and pepper

Preheat oven to 400°.

Peel corn down to last 2 layers of husk. Fold back these last 2 layers and remove corn silk. Pull the husk back up and rub each with the corn oil. Roast corn in oven for ½ hour. Let the corn cool down a bit and then peel off the husk. Grill the corn for 3 minutes on each side. Brush with melted butter, season with salt and pepper.

Corn Bread

4 cups cornmeal	1 tablespoon sugar
4 cups all-purpose flour	8 eggs
2 teaspoons baking powder	4½ cups sour cream
3 teaspoons salt	½ cup unsalted butter, soft

Preheat oven to 400°.

In a large bowl, mix all dry ingredients. Form a well in center of bowl. Beat in eggs and sour cream until smooth.

Grease 2 large, cast-iron pans (or 2 cookie sheets) with butter. Pour equal amounts of batter into pans, filling ¾ full.

Bake 15 to 20 minutes. The top should be a golden brown. A knife, when inserted in middle, should come out clean.

Focaccia Salad

This salad can be made the day before the cookout. If you decide to prepare this early, just remember to set the focaccia croutons aside and fold them into the salad just before serving.

5 cucumbers, peeled, seeded, diced	2 lb. fresh mozzarella, diced
10 plum tomatoes, seeded, quartered	3 cups olive oil
2 red onions, peeled, diced	½ cup red wine vinegar
10 basil leaves, julienned	½ cup balsamic vinegar
1 teaspoon garlic, sliced	1 8" focaccia round, plain

Mix all ingredients except focaccia into a large bowl.

Preheat oven to 350°. To make the croutons, cut the focaccia into ½" cubes. Toast croutons for 10 minutes. Fold into salad just before serving.

Potato Salad

8 lb. red potatoes, size B
2 tablespoons olive oil
15 cloves garlic, peeled
12 hard-boiled eggs, peeled, chopped
1 cup celery, diced
1 bunch rosemary

1 cup onion, diced
1 cup Dijon mustard
4 cups mayonnaise
1 tablespoon sugar
1 tablespoon white vinegar
Salt and pepper

Scrub potatoes, quarter, place in large stockpot with enough water to cover, and boil for 25 to 30 minutes. Drain through colander and set aside.

Heat olive oil in a sauté pan, add garlic, and simmer at low heat for 25 to 30 minutes or until soft. Remove from heat and let cool. Puree garlic and set aside.

To prepare the hard-boiled eggs, place eggs in a large stockpot with enough cold water to cover. Bring to a boil and cook for 12 minutes. When finished, immediately transfer eggs to a pan filled with ice water. Let the eggs sit in the ice water for 10 minutes, adding ice as needed. This will prevent discoloration of eggs and make them easier to peel. Drain, peel, and chop eggs. Set aside.

Chop 1 tablespoon of rosemary. Set aside.

In a large bowl, combine all ingredients.

Garnish with remaining sprigs of rosemary.

Strawberry Shortcake

4 qt. strawberries
2 cups sugar
Zest of 4 lemons

Juice of 1 lemon
2 cups water

Clean, remove stems, and quarter the strawberries. Set aside.

In a small saucepan, mix all other ingredients and bring to a boil. Remove from heat when liquid becomes clear. Strain the syrup into a bowl and set aside.

One hour before serving, toss strawberries with the syrup and let sit at room temperature.

THE SHORTCAKE

8 cups cake flour
3 tablespoons baking powder
½ cup confectioners' sugar
1 tablespoon plus 1 teaspoon salt
6 oz. unsalted butter

6 oz. Crisco
4 eggs
2½ cups milk
¼ cup granulated sugar

Preheat oven to 400°.

Into a bowl, sift and combine first four ingredients. Cut butter and Crisco into dry mixture, using your fingers, until it resembles coarse meal.

In a separate bowl, lightly beat eggs and 2 cups milk together. Add this to flour mixture and combine thoroughly.

Place dough on lightly floured surface and knead until silky and smooth. If dough sticks to surface, sprinkle with more flour. Roll out dough ¾" thick. Using a 3" round cutter, cut out 24 shortcakes. Place rounds 1" apart on lightly greased cookie sheets. Lightly brush each round with remaining milk and sprinkle with granulated sugar.

Bake for 10 to 12 minutes or until golden brown.

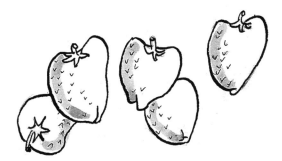

All Hallows' Eve Garlic Frenzy
(A Kissing Party for Twelve)

MENU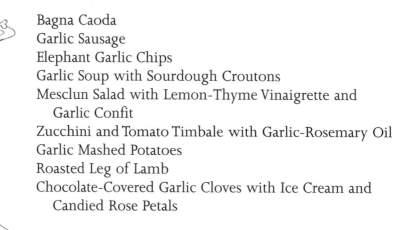

Bagna Caoda
Garlic Sausage
Elephant Garlic Chips
Garlic Soup with Sourdough Croutons
Mesclun Salad with Lemon-Thyme Vinaigrette and
    Garlic Confit
Zucchini and Tomato Timbale with Garlic-Rosemary Oil
Garlic Mashed Potatoes
Roasted Leg of Lamb
Chocolate-Covered Garlic Cloves with Ice Cream and
    Candied Rose Petals

**GAMES AND
THINGS**

Garlic Guess-Off
Fuzzy Duck
Bobbing for Garlic
Black Magic
Ouija!

COCKTAILS

Bloody Jack

CRAFTS

Garlic Necklace Invitations
Scary Shrunken Apple Heads
Pumpkin Totem Pole Centerpiece
Cute Vegetable Critters

If Ed Wood and Bela Lugosi had invited Martha Stewart over for dinner, it might have ended up a little bit like this. This is a traditional Halloween party to celebrate the natural ghoulishness of the day. Have your friends dress up as an incarnation of their dark side.

Halloween, or Samhain in Celtic, is the day of the year when the veil between the physical world and the spirit world is at its thinnest point, so if you feel a need to chat with some long-gone ancestors, this would be the time. The evil spirit aspect of Halloween has been blown way out of proportion. In the spirit world, you've got your good and your bad, the same as in the physical world. So on Halloween, when your late, great Aunt Mary breezes in through the window to pay you a call, she might bring with her a little unwanted riffraff. That's where the garlic comes in.

Garlic purifies the blood, and it's thought to have properties that purify the atmosphere from bad vibes. With all the garlic you'll have around your house, Aunt Mary is going to have to tell her bad-boy spirit friends to wait for her on the corner.

In addition to cleaning things out, garlic is also said to have special powers as an aphrodisiac. Legend has it that in India, men make a mixture of garlic and fat and spread it on their penises in order to maintain an erection for hours on end. I think Jack may be experimenting with this. We'll be sure to let you know how it goes.

For extra fun, tell just one of the guests to dress as a vampire. As usual, when we threw our party, we didn't really think the whole thing through in advance. We thought, oh, garlic, vampires, great. Then we realized that you use garlic to keep the vampires away. It was too late. We had already told one of the guests to dress as one, and we forgot to inform him otherwise. Everyone was quite delighted when he arrived at the door in a cape and fangs— everyone but him, that is.

The beauty of a garlic party is that after our five-course garlic extravaganza, no one is going to want to go out disco dancing, so take advantage of your captive guests and play fuzzy duck, our little a-drinkin'-and-a-kissin' game. One word of caution, though: If you want to try the kissing game, be sure you think the guest list through ahead of time, and instead of inviting the same old queens that come to all of your parties, include a little fresh blood. Otherwise, it's a bit incestuous—which might be fun, depending on your personal proclivities.

Later, if you still feel like going out, get Aunt Mary's ghost and drive her back home to the local cemetery. While you're there, visit with all those others who have passed over into the netherworld, and bring them some leftover garlic chips.

Miss Party Fabulous Warns: Our guests reported complaints from coworkers the day after our party, so you might want to have yours on a Saturday so your guests have a whole day to air out before returning to the office.

Garlic Necklace Invitations

Since this party is on that mother of all dress-up holidays, the invitation is going to be something that your guests can wear to the party. Something that will make them stand out from all the other goblins that are milling around the streets. It also has the added purpose of warding off any vampires that may have designs on the tender flesh of their necks—a garlic necklace.

YOU'LL NEED

Twelve heads of garlic
Twelve leather thongs about 2 feet long
Twelve pieces of black paper, 3" × 5"
Twelve boxes that will be able to accommodate one head of garlic each
Twelve pieces of black lace to wrap the treasured necklace
Silver marking pen

- Find something that you can use to insert a hole through a head of garlic like an awl, a skinny screwdriver, or even an ice pick.
- Make the hole.
- Then fold one end of a leather thong over your boring tool and stick it through the hole again. Voilà! You've got garlic on a string.
- Tie the ends together and you've got a garlic necklace.
- Now, on your black paper, use the silver marker to write all the pertinent information for your party, making sure to note that the necklaces must be worn to gain entrance to the party.

- Fold and place at the bottom of your box.
- Delicately swath the necklace in the fabric and place in the box.
- Close up the boxes, send them out, and you're on your way to throwing a garlic frenzy.

crafts

The crafts for this party are our most organic—literally. They're all made from items purchased at your local greengrocer. There's the lovely pumpkin totem pole centerpiece, the cute and wacky vegetable critters, and the scary shrunken apple heads. Even the invitation, the garlic necklace, was once part of Mother Earth.

Scary Shrunken Apple Heads

These you'll need to make ahead of time because they need at least a week or so to shrink into their scariest forms.

YOU'LL NEED

Apples
A paring knife
Some twine

- Now we can begin. Peel your apples.
- Then carve them into the shapes of different heads. Use people you know as models: your boss, an old boyfriend, or anyone whose head you might like to see shriveled and shrunken. Also don't be subtle. Make a big mouth or very deep-set eyes, because by the end of the week, that big mouth is going to look like a little shriveled pucker.
- Hang them in that root cellar (that's where the twine comes in) and wait.
- In about a week or so, you'll have scary shrunken apple heads to place around your house. Put them near candles because the flickering light will make them even scarier.

Unfortunately, we didn't have a root cellar the first time we made these at the Grill. As usual, we started late, so to speed up the drying process, we popped our apples in the oven overnight. The next morning; the chef turned the oven up to 400 degrees without removing our little apples. Instead of looking like scary shrunken apple heads, they turned into blackened little chunks of charcoal.

Pumpkin Totem Pole Centerpiece

You should make this the morning of the party because its shelf life is limited.

YOU'LL NEED

3 small pumpkins of varying sizes
3 votive candles
A good sturdy knife

This is an easy one, as everyone has carved a pumpkin. What you'll need to remember is that since this is a centerpiece, you'll need to carve all around the pumpkins. After the carving is through, arrange them one on top of the other with the biggest on the bottom and the smallest on top. Just before the guests arrive, light it up. Your guests will be talking about it for weeks.

Cute Vegetable Critters

These are the most fun, because you get to browse at the greengrocer and pick the weirdest-shaped vegetables and the cashier won't quite know what to make of you.

YOU'LL NEED

A variety of oddly shaped vegetables
Construction paper
Scissors
Glue
A felt-tip pen
Toothpicks

- First thing to do is study your vegetables. What is it? What's it saying to you? Is it a snake, a penguin, or just a nutty-looking head?
- Using your construction paper make some accessories like a hat or tie. Big black eyelashes are a favorite. This is kind of like making your own Mr. Potato Head only it's a mutated carrot or deformed pepper.
- Attach the accessories with glue and use your felt-tip pen to make some eyes or whatever other features you want.
- Three toothpicks come in handy when you need a base for a wobbly bell pepper. Stick three in the base of your critter like a tripod and it will wobble no more.
- Place your critters around the centerpiece, and as the dinner progresses you'll notice that the spirits that are being invoked by the Ouija start to inhabit your critters (or was that just the garlic vodka?).

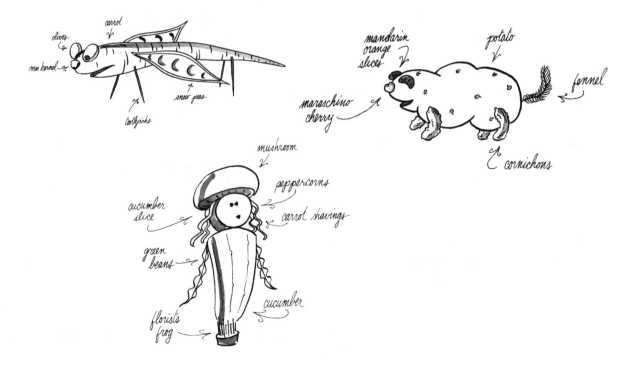

Garlic Guess-Off This is the icebreaker game. When your guests come in, hand them a big old Bloody Jack, then show them the way to the table, where in the midst of your vegetable critter centerpiece, you have a lovely head of garlic prominently displayed. (If you want to be really chichi, you can spray-paint this special head gold for added glitz and glamour.) Have your guests guess the number of cloves contained in the orb, and write their name and their guess on a piece of paper. Collect the papers. Then, after dinner but before dessert, crack the head open, count out the cloves, and award the winner with the special garlic crown you've made for him or her.

Fuzzy Duck Get a ball, a wad of socks, or even a spare head of garlic, and sit your group down in a circle on the floor. One person begins by tossing the object to another and saying, "Fuzzy duck." The receiver responds with, "Ducky fuzz," and tosses it to another person, who responds with, "Fuzzy duck," etc. As you continue, speed up the pace. Eventually, someone will mess up and invert a few letters, and that's when the kissing or drinking comes in. The messer-upper must kiss whoever threw the object to him or her in the kissing version (we call that the Jack version of the game) or take a swig from the bottle in the drinking version (obviously the Todd version of the game). If you are democratic by nature, you can allow the person to choose, but the best version by far is to play it both ways at the same time: take a swig and then pucker up.

Miss Party Fabulous Says: Don't forget the Glade air freshener, the Clorets, and the Listerine.

Bobbing for Garlic

We love this game because you get to see all your friends bobbing around with their mouths open, like blind baby chicks in a feeding frenzy.

You'll need about a dozen large heads of garlic, some cord, a big needle, and some scarves or dinner napkins to blindfold the players. What you're going to do is thread a length of cord through each head of garlic and suspend them from the ceiling so that they hang approximately at mouth level. Mouth level varies from person to person, so you'll have to have some varying lengths. Hang four at a time, then choose four players. Blindfold them, spin them around and get them all dizzy, then holler "Go!" The object is to be the first one to grab a head of garlic in your mouth.

Why not just bob for apples in a washtub, you ask? 'Cause this way ya don't ruin your hairdo, girlfriend.

Black Magic

This is a little party trick that's lots of fun. You'll need to set it up beforehand with a buddy.

After dinner, when you're all still sitting around the table trying not to belch, you mention that you and your friend, who we'll call Joe, have a special psychic connection. It's the strangest thing, you say, but you can sometimes read his mind! Then you offer to demonstrate. You leave the room, and Joe tells the other guests to agree upon one object in the room. Then you come back and sit across from Joe. Act spooky, like you're really concentrating on getting the vibe. Joe will ask if you're ready, you'll say yes, and Joe will begin. He'll say, "Is it this glass?" "Is it this chair?" etc., pointing to the objects as he goes along. Finally he'll come to the object, and you, being psychic, will say, "Yes!!! *Yes*! It is definitely that!"

The trick is simple. Whatever the object is, Joe will point to something black immediately before pointing to the object. For instance, if the object is an old wig, Joe will point to someone's black-rimmed glasses and say, "Is it the frames of these glasses?" right before he asks, "Is it this old wig here on the floor?"

Once you've mastered that, you're ready for part two. You tell your astonished friends that sometimes, but not always, you are able do the same thing with names—names of famous people, friends, whoever. Once again you leave the room, and the group decides on a name. We'll use Donald Duck. When you come back, you listen very carefully to what Joe says. Joe is going to act like he's conjuring a feeling here, but what he's really doing is *spelling out the name for you by starting each sentence with a letter from the name*. For the vowels, Joe claps, snaps his fingers, or pounds on the table, using one beat for *A*, two for *E*, three for *I*, four for *O*, and five for *U*. (Treat Y like a consonant.) So for Donald Duck, Joe says something like, "Delicately clear your mind," then he claps four times for the *O*. "Now, are you starting to feel it?" he asks, then pounds on the table once for the *A*. "Listen to the vibrations!" "Do not let your mind wander!" "Digest all the sounds!" Five more claps, for the *U*. Joe continues for the *C* and the *K*, but by then, you'll probably have it. You can start acting spooky, saying things like, "I hear a quack." Then you jump to your feet and pronounce, "Donald Duck!"

Ouija!

Mystifying oracle! Set the mood for this after-dinner game by turning the lights down low and lighting some extra candles. Place the Ouija board right on the dinner table or in a quiet corner. Let your guests reach the other side, bring back the dead or pick some winning lotto numbers.

Miss Party Fabulous Says: If guests start disappearing, speaking in tongues or flying through windows it's time to start bobbing for garlic again!

Andy Williams
Honey
Columbia Records
"Spooky"

Donovan
Sunshine Superman
Epic
"Season of the Witch"

Bubby (Boris) Pickett
*The Monster Mash
and Monster Mash Party*
London Recordings, 45 rpm

Liza Minelli
You're So Vain
Columbia
"Dancing in the Moonlight"

Louis Prima and Keely Smith
*Plaza House Presents a
Collectors Limited
Edition: The Greatest Hits of the
'50s and '60s*
"That Old Black Magic"

Jim Nabors
By Request
Columbia Records
"Sunrise, Sunset"

Tee Vee Presents Television's
Greatest Hits—66 TV Themes!
"The Munsters" and **"The
Addams Family"**

The Rocky Horror Picture Show
Sound Track

Disneyland Records Presents:
*Chilling, Thrilling Sounds of the
Haunted House*
"Chinese Water Torture" and
"Cat Fight"

Diva
Sound Track
DRG Records
"Ground Swell"

Jaws Sound Track
MCA Records, 1975
**"Main Title (Theme from
Jaws)"**

Steve Martin and the Toot
Uncommons
Warner Bros. Records, 1977
"King Tut," 45 rpm

cocktails

Bloody Jack

The drink of choice for this smelly event is one that packs a punch and sets the mood—and breath—for the rest of the evening: the Bloody Jack. Forget those fey lemon-flavored designer vodkas. The only flavor that will do to keep the vampires (and everyone else) away is *garlic*.

YOU'LL NEED

One Head of garlic, peeled
One bottle of good vodka

Take the bottle of vodka and pour off a couple of shots. Set these aside for future consumption. Put the peeled cloves into the bottle and stick it in the freezer for at least 48 hours. That's it!

THE MIX

One can of V8 juice
Two heaping, heaping tablespoons of horseradish
Eight shakes of the Worcestershire sauce bottle
Five shakes of Tabasco
Four turns of the pepper mill
Juice of half a lemon
Two shakes of celery salt (the Merrell family secret ingredient)

Try not to make it too spicy, 'cause you want to taste that garlic! Mix it all together and drink up. Although everybody will probably be clamoring for more Bloody Jacks, wine is probably better with dinner. But if they insist, don't hold back. Give them all the Bloody Jacks they can handle!

Bagna Caoda

2 cups peeled garlic cloves
2 cups olive oil
4 anchovy fillets

In a large saucepan, heat the garlic cloves and olive oil. Simmer at low heat for 25 to 30 minutes or until garlic is soft. Remove from heat and let cool. Add the anchovies. In a food processor, puree all ingredients until smooth.

Best served in a fondue pot with toast points or julienned vegetables.

Garlic Sausage

If you're ambitious and have your own sausage grinder and casings, by all means, grind that meat and stuff that sausage! For convenience, we suggest you purchase 5 to 6 links of dried garlic sausage from your butcher. All you do is remove the casing, thinly slice, and tastefully arrange the sausage around a mound of garlic chips on a lovely platter. Be sure to have a small dish of Dijon mustard on the side. No muss, no fuss, and tasty, too.

Miss Party Fabulous Says: For this party, you will need 558 cloves of garlic. Unless you've got a gaggle of peasants working for you, we suggest you buy a quart container of cloves, prepeeled.

Elephant Garlic Chips

1 qt. peanut oil
2 heads of elephant garlic, peeled
Salt and pepper to taste

In a large pot, heat the peanut oil to 350°.

Use a deep-fry thermometer to check temperature. You can also test the oil by throwing in one garlic chip: if it sizzles and floats, the oil is ready.

While the oil is heating, thinly slice the garlic. Deep-fry garlic until edges are brown. Remove chips from oil with a slotted spoon and place on paper towels to drain. Season with salt and pepper.

Garlic Soup with Sourdough Croutons

150 cloves blanched garlic
2 leeks, sliced (white part only)
2 celery stalks, sliced
4 oz. unsalted butter
4 qt. chicken stock
   (see recipe on page 21)

2 cloves (not garlic; the other aromatic)
2 Idaho potatoes, peeled, thinly sliced
Salt and pepper
2 bunches sage, chopped
Sourdough croutons

This recipe calls for a lot of garlic, which you will need to blanch ahead of time—not the most difficult task in the world, just slightly boring. In a medium saucepan, boil 2 quarts of water, then add the garlic. When the water returns to a boil, remove from heat and drain cloves through a colander in the sink. Repeat this process two more times. This softens the garlic and removes the heat or burning sensation of the raw cloves. Let the soup begin!

In a medium-size stockpot, sauté leeks and celery in butter. Add stock and cloves, and bring to a boil. Add potatoes and garlic. Simmer for 45 minutes to 1 hour or until all is soft.

Using a stick blender or food processor, puree soup until smooth. Season with salt and pepper.

Garnish with chopped sage and sourdough croutons.

SOURDOUGH CROUTONS

1 sourdough baguette
½ lb. butter

Preheat oven to 350°.

Select a nice, soft sourdough baguette. While the oven is heating, slice or dice the baguette. In a saucepan, melt the butter, into which you will dip and coat each crouton. On a cookie sheet, arrange the croutons, being careful not to overlap them. Toast croutons in oven for 5 to 7 minutes.

Mesclun Salad with Lemon-Thyme Vinaigrette and Garlic Confit

Mesclun is a wonderful mixture of baby lettuce leaves. Purchased by the pound, mesclun is made up of eleven to sixteen different kinds of lettuce, including arugula, chervil, lamb's lettuce, and oak leaf. If you're the gardening type and prefer to mix your own greens, you can go wild and throw in some mizuna or dandelion leaves. Use baby greens that are fresh, tender, and succulent.

For this party, you will need 2 pounds of mesclun, which should be thoroughly washed and dried. Toss greens with vinaigrette, taking care to get a light, even coating. Arrange greens on salad plates and garnish each with 4 to 5 cloves of garlic confit. Drizzle just a bit of the remaining vinaigrette on each salad.

LEMON-THYME VINAIGRETTE

Zest of 2 lemons
2 cups canola oil
½ cup rice wine vinegar

1 bunch of thyme, chopped
Salt and pepper

To obtain lemon zest, grate lemon rind on a cheese grater.

Whisk oil and vinegar together. Add lemon zest, thyme, and salt and pepper to taste.

Vinaigrette is best when made the day before and refrigerated overnight.

GARLIC CONFIT

2 cups peeled garlic cloves
2 cups olive oil
1 cup bread crumbs

In a saucepan, heat the garlic cloves and olive oil. Simmer at low heat for 25 to 30 minutes or until garlic is soft. Remove from heat and let cool. With a slotted spoon, remove garlic cloves from oil and roll them in bread crumbs.

Set aside and use as garnish for salad.

Zucchini and Tomato Timbale with Garlic-Rosemary Oil

5 large zucchini
15 plum tomatoes
Salt and pepper

Garlic-rosemary oil
½ cup grated parmesan

To assemble the timbales, you can use either individual molds or a large muffin tin. We've found that Teflon-coated tins work best.

Preheat oven to 350°.

Very thinly slice the zucchini and the plum tomatoes on a bias, i.e., olive shape. Season with salt and pepper and set aside.

Rub each mold with 1 oz. of the garlic-rosemary oil.

Place one slice of zucchini at the bottom of each mold. Cut this slice of zucchini to fit exactly into the bottom of the mold. If you're feeling artistic, create a design such as a star or crescent, which will crown the timbale when unmolded.

Alternate slices of zucchini and tomato around sides of mold, until mold is tightly packed. Sprinkle each timbale with more of the oil and the grated parmesan. Bake the timbales for 1 hour. Let sit for 25 minutes before unmolding.

GARLIC-ROSEMARY OIL

1 qt. olive oil
5 heads of garlic, split
5 sprigs fresh rosemary

In a large saucepan, slowly heat the olive oil and garlic. When the garlic starts to sizzle, remove from heat. Add rosemary. Cover pan with lid and let sit overnight at room temperature.

On the following day, strain oil into a glass pitcher or jar.

Garlic Mashed Potatoes

10 Idaho potatoes
20 cloves garlic
1½ qt. milk

½ lb. unsalted butter
Salt and pepper

Thoroughly scrub potatoes. Place potatoes in a large stockpot and cover with cold water. Bring to a boil and then reduce heat to simmer. Add garlic cloves. Simmer for 15 to 20 minutes or until potatoes are very soft. Drain potatoes and garlic into a colander, then return to stockpot. Add the milk and butter. With a potato masher, mash until smooth. For creamier mashed potatoes, add more milk to obtain desired consistency. Season with salt and pepper.

Roasted Leg of Lamb

Have your butcher bone and tie two legs of lamb. Also, ask for the bones to be split; you'll need them for roasting.

2 5-lb. legs of lamb	1 carrot, coarsely chopped
4 tablespoons chopped garlic	1 celery stalk, coarsely chopped
Juice of 2 lemons	1 bunch tarragon
4 cups veal stock	1 bunch thyme
(see recipe on page 76)	1 bay leaf
6 oz. olive oil	Salt and pepper
1 leek, coarsely chopped	

The day before the party, rub the leg of lamb with the garlic and lemon. Cover and refrigerate overnight. You can also prepare the veal stock ahead of time.

Now you're ready to begin preparing the lamb.

Preheat oven to 450°.

On the stove, in a roasting pan, heat 4 oz. olive oil. Brown the lamb on all sides. Remove lamb from pan and set aside.

In the roasting pan, heat the remaining olive oil and brown sliced bones. This will take 2 to 3 minutes. Remove from heat. Add the chopped vegetables to the roasting pan. Set the lamb on top of the bones and vegetables. Place the pan in the oven and roast until meat thermometer reads 130° (about 1 hour and 15 minutes). As everyone's oven is different, the meat thermometer is the most accurate tool in determining the cooking time. At 130°, your lamb should come out medium.

Remove pan from oven and set aside only the lamb.

Place the pan on the stove, and to the bones and vegetables add the veal stock, any drippings from the lamb, and the herbs. Bring this to a boil and then simmer until reduced by half. Skim off the grease and foam that forms on top.

While the jus is reducing, slice the lamb very thin. Don't forget to slice against the grain of the meat. After slicing, add any remaining drippings to jus. Arrange lamb on a platter. Strain the jus into a bowl and season with salt and pepper. Serve on the side.

Miss Party Fabulous Says: Get to know your butcher; he can be your best friend. We all remember Alice and Sam the butcher from *The Brady Bunch*. Not only did she get the finest cold cuts, but an occasional night on the town.

Chocolate-Covered Garlic Cloves with Ice Cream and Candied Rose Petals

If you've had chocolate-covered ants or chocolate-covered pretzels, you're gonna love chocolate-covered garlic cloves. Your guests may think your brain is covered in chocolate, but they'll soon be toasting you as the hostess with the garlic mostest.

60 cloves garlic, blanched
2 oz. unsalted butter, melted
1 lb. Calabaut chocolate, semisweet
½ gal. vanilla ice cream

Small box candied rose petals (or violets)
1 bunch mint
Powdered sugar

To blanch garlic cloves, see recipe for garlic soup on page 164. If you're using both recipes for this dinner, just use a larger pot and blanch them all together.

Preheat oven to 350°.

Toss the garlic cloves with the melted butter. Place the cloves on a cookie sheet and roast in oven for 40 minutes or until brown. Be sure to turn them after the first 20 minutes in the oven. Set aside to cool and then place tray in refrigerator.

Break chocolate into small pieces. Set aside 2 oz. of chocolate for tempering. In a double boiler, melt chocolate until smooth (about 10 to 12 minutes). Remove from heat. While stirring, slowly add remaining 2 oz. of unmelted chocolate. This will temper your chocolate and cause it to harden properly. Dip garlic cloves into the tempered chocolate using either a fork or skewer. Place on a tray covered with wax paper and cool in refrigerator.

When you're ready to serve dessert, scoop vanilla ice cream onto a cold plate. Garlic ice cream does exist; if you can find it, substitute it for vanilla. Garnish with the chocolate covered garlic cloves (5 per serving), and candied rose petals (or violets). Throw on a few sprigs of mint and just a whisp of powdered sugar. Delicious.

TEN WAYS TO WHIP A CROWD INTO A FRENZY

1. Take your cues from them. When you put an album on, look for your guests' response.
2. Once you get a response, mine the same vein for a few songs, then change the tempo, the decade, the genre. This is where your intuition comes into play.
3. When people respond, don't be afraid to crank it.
4. Mix the familiar with the obscure. Segue from *The Sound of Music* sound track to Joan Jett doing "I Love Rock 'n' Roll."
5. Dance. That's right. Get up and lead the way. Conga out one door and in the other. Rhumba till you drop. Watusi till the cows come home. (Lampshades optional.)

6. Keep the booze flowing.
7. Now it's time for props. Wigs, bras, tambourines, outrageous costume jewelry, a tiara—be sure and have some of these on hand.
8. Scan the room for someone who is either deeply grooving to the music or doing an impromptu performance on the dance floor. Take your handy spotlight (a high-powered flashlight will do) and shine a light on him or her.
9. Throw caution to the winds and dance on the furniture. Go from the chairs to the dining room table, but draw the line at swinging from the chandelier! That's only for the movies, girlfriend.
10. When all else fails, *strip!* Caution: This could make or break your party!

A Night at Studio 54
(A Different Kind of Halloween Party for Sixty)

MENU Assortment of candy and snack foods that resemble drugs

GAMES AND THINGS Guess Who the Guest Is Supposed to Be
Dance Contest

COCKTAILS Full Bar!

CRAFTS The Pill Bottle Invitation
The Famous Studio 54 Icons
The Bags of Money

Studio 54 holds a special place in the hearts of all who were lucky enough to have passed through its portals. It even resonates for those who never made it there but fondly recall reading about it in their dusty hometowns, longing for the day when they, too, could buy a pair of platform shoes and join the crowd at the velvet ropes, hoping to be one of the chosen few. It was a fantasyland where high brow and low brow mixed and intermingled. With Andy, Mick, and Liza in attendance, anything was possible. You could be Cinderella and be swept away by a fabulous prince. Or, if you were a fabulous prince, you could pick up a sexy mechanic, just to see how the other half lived. It was a place where fairy tales could come true or explode on a nightly basis.

But how do I transform a little one-bedroom into a glamorous star-studded discotheque? You may ask. Through rentals, of course! We're not talking about Hertz or Avis, honey. For this create-a-disco-in-your-own-home party, we recommend that you rent a light system, sound system, and a fog machine. As your walls disappear behind a dense, white, piña colada–scented fog, you'll see your little home or apartment metamorphose into a pulsating discotheque, circa 1976. All this renting may seem excessive, but believe us, it's worth it. Just think of the expressions on your neighbors' faces when they see your house transformed into a mirage of light, smoke, and sound. If you've gone this far, why not go the whole way and rent some velvet ropes? It's always fun to make your invitation-holding friends wait outside while you decide who to let in first.

"Give energy," was the mantra of one of the Studio door people, and that really is the essence of the Studio 54 experience. Energy, whether natural or chemically induced, will make or break this night, so go all the way, don't hold back, and let yourself believe that this single night can change the rest of your life. After all, if you believe it, baby, maybe it'll come true. Say, isn't that Bianca coming through the front door on a white horse right now?

Miss Party Fabulous Asks: How do you know when you've had a few too many? When your voice reaches a decibel appropriate for an airplane hangar, but you're actually in a studio apartment.

invitations

The Pill Bottle Invitation

Disco, hedonistic sex, and . . . drugs. Oh that Studio. It would be hard to make an invitation that made one think of disco and it would just be in bad taste to send out sex, but I bet we can come up with something that can be sent (legally) in the mail that would evoke our third thought of Studio 54. How about a pill bottle? The kind our neighborhood pharmacist gives out every day at the local pharmacy. Of course, the bottle will hold Tic Tacs, not bennies. If your guests want something stronger, they'll have to find it themselves.

YOU'LL NEED

Sixty 2" × 2" white labels
Sixty pill bottles
Breath mints (Tic Tacs are just right)
One roll of cotton
Sixty small, padded mailing envelopes

- To get your information on your label, the ideal situation would be that you have a computer that has a label template. Your worries would be about the font size and centering and you would have to concentrate on the making of the very first one and then just copy-paste, copy-paste, copy-paste. But alas, that is probably not an option for some of you, so you'll have to get out that ol' trusty typewriter.
- Here's how the copy should look:

THE YOUR NAME PHARMACY
Your address

Patient's(Guest's) Name

Patient will take one dose of
Studio 54 every half hour on Oct.
31 starting at 9:00 p.m.

For prescription to be effective,
proper disco attire is required. No
exceptions.

- Stick each label onto each pill bottle.
- Fill each bottle with about 10 Tic Tacs.
- Top it off with a chunk of cotton and recap.
- Then just send them off in the mailing envelopes.

The resurrection of Studio 54 will soon be upon you.

crafts

The Famous Studio 54 Icons

For this descent into the decadent decade of disco, the crafts will come from the images that were burned into our brains from too many nights at the ultimate den of dance fever: Studio 54. The images are definitely not PC, because PC didn't exist back then. There were the icons that dropped from the ceiling when a particular song hit a frenzied, fevered pitch. There was the white horse that Bianca Jagger rode in on for her birthday party. And there were the rumored bags of money that were kept in various nooks and crannies around the club. That should keep us busy. After all, if we can recreate enough of the ambiance of Studio, nobody's going to remember much for a couple of weeks.

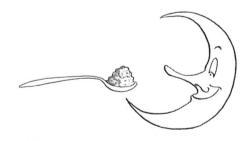

YOU'LL NEED
Six pieces of 30" × 40" foam core
One box cutter
Assorted spray paint (silver and bright red)
Glitter (bright red and silver)
One thick black felt-tip pen
Elmer's glue
Two sheets of 12" × 18" white construction paper
One sheet of 8½" × 11" beige construction paper
Tape
Fishing wire
Staple gun

- For each of the icons that we're going to make, we're going to double the recipe and make two. That way, they should be represented throughout the house so that some reminiscence of Studio 54 will be in someone's view practically all the time.
- Of course, the most remembered icon that fell from the ceiling is probably also the one that is the least politically correct for the nineties. Hey, but we're just being retro here, right? And to think of all the big politicians that went to Studio then. This icon is the man in the moon with a coke spoon.
- For this, which consists of two separate pieces—the moon and the spoon— we're going to use two pieces of foam core.
- First we're going to tackle the man. Take one of the sheets of foam core and cut it into two 30" × 20" pieces. Each piece will be used for one of the men in the moon.
- From the rendition shown, draw a man in the moon, trying to use as much of the surface as possible. Don't worry if you screw up the first try, it's going to be spray-painted, anyway.
- When you think you've got the image down to your satisfaction, cut it out using your box cutter. Make sure you cut it out on a piece of old plywood or in the garage: it's horrible when you start scratching up the linoleum in the kitchen.

- Place the man over the other piece of foam core and trace.
- Then cut out the second. The image of the man is complete, though not completed.
- Cut another piece of foam core in half as you did before. One of these sheets will be used for the two spoons.
- Use the image shown as a basis and draw two spoons.
- Cut them out.
- Now, we're going to spray-paint them with our silver spray paint.
- When that is completely dry, we need to add on the final touches with our glitter and felt-tip pen.
- On the man in the moon, you will need to outline with your felt-tip pen an eye, the lips, and most importantly, the nostril.
- For the spoon, you will just need to make it a little 3-D by outlining the bowl.
- Now, squirt some Elmer's around the nostril and then sprinkle on the silver glitter. Shake off the excess and let dry. Do the same in the bowl of the spoon. And there you have the man in the moon with a coke spoon. We'll hang them up later, after we have the others made.
- The next icon is a big pair of juicy red lips holding a lit cigarette.
- We'll start by cutting one of the pieces of foam core in half just as we did before.
- On the first piece, draw a pair of lips.
- Cut them out.
- Trace them onto the other piece.
- Cut them out.
- Then spray paint them red.
- Use the felt-tip pen to draw the line where the lips meet.
- Dribble on the Elmer's so that a lot of the lip is covered and then pour on the red glitter. Shake off the excess. Voilà—lips.
- Take the white construction paper and roll it so that you end up with a tube 18" long and 2" in diameter.
- Tape the edges.

- Cut the beige construction paper into two pieces that are 8½" × 5½".
- Roll one piece around the end of the white cylinder so that it looks like the filter of a cigarette. Tape together.
- Drizzle Elmer's onto the other end and sprinkle on a mixture of the silver and red glitter.
- In the center of the lips, cut a hole that is two inches in diameter.
- Stick the cigarette into the hole so that 2" has been exposed behind. To attach the cigarette, make 4 incisions around the cigarette filter end and then flatten these to the back of the lips. Tape on.
- Now it's time to hang them up using the fishing wire. Make a small hole in the top of each icon and thread the fishing line through. The length is pretty much dependent on the size of your ceilings. Staple gun to the ceiling and you're looking like you live in a disco.

The Bags of Money

YOU'LL NEED   Six medium, dark green garbage bags
Loads of old newspaper (enough to fill the garbage bags)
Play money
Glue

- Fill each of the bags with shredded newspaper.
- Loosely tie off the bags, leaving 4" at the top.
- Take the play money and glue to the inside of the top of the bag.
- The image should be of gobs of money overflowing out of the bags.
- Place the bags conspicuously throughout your apartment, i.e., under the bed but slightly sticking out, in a cupboard, under the bathroom sink. Just hope none of your guests work for the IRS.

Guess Who the Guest Is Supposed to Be

An optional aspect of this party is to ask your guests to dress up as their favorite denizen of Studio 54. If you choose to do that, then you can make a little game out of guessing who is supposed to be who. Have different prizes for different categories. A little trophy for the guest whose getup is most convincing, and a certificate for a makeover for the guest who is farthest off the mark. Other possible categories are Most Creative, Best Cross-Gender Costume, Best Same-Sex Costume, etc., etc. You get the idea.

Dance Contest

This one isn't really a contest, and it isn't really, truly Studio 54, either. Remember on Soul Train, when the dancers would make two lines facing each other and then take turns dancing down the middle? Give it a try; it brings out everybody's exhibitionistic side and really gets things going.

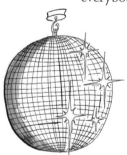

A Night at Studio 54
Casablanca Records, 1979

Viola Wills
If You Could Read My Mind
Arista, 1980
"(There's) Always Something There to Remind Me"

Van McCoy and the Soul City Symphony
Disco Baby
Avco Records, 1975
"The Hustle"

Meca
Star Wars and Other Galactic Funk
Millennium, 1977

Dr. Buzzards's Original Savannah Band
RCA Records, 1976
"Cherchez la Femme"

The Ethel Merman Disco Album
A&M Records, 1979
"There's No Business Like Show Business"

Vicki Sue Robinson
Never Gonna Let You Go
RCA Records, 1976
"Turn the Beat Around"

Liza Minnelli
The Singer
Columbia
"You're So Vain"

Sister Sledge
We Are Family
Cotillion Records, 1979

Grace Jones
Portfolio
Island Records, 1976
"La Vie en Rose"

Michael Jackson
Off the Wall
Epic Records, 1979

Rick James
Street Songs
Gordy
"Super Freak"

Festival
Evita
RSO Records, 1979
"Don't Cry for Me Argentina"

Donna Summer/ Barbra Streisand
Casablanca Records, 1979
"No More Tears (Enough Is Enough)"

cocktails

Full Bar!

There is no real cocktail that can be associated with Studio 54. Drugs . . . maybe. But everyone drinks what they want at a disco. So for this party we're going to concentrate on the bar. Since the disco is in your own house, the bar should be streamlined, giving the revelers a choice but not every liquor under the sun. Our home bar is so streamlined, in fact, that there is basically just beer, wine, and vodka. This came about after years of giving parties and the realization hit that our friends will drink anything you give them. For you, with a more discerning stable of friends, we'll set up a well-stocked but lean bar. The first thing to understand when setting up your bar is your guests. Who has a very particular drink? Is there anyone who only drinks scotch with milk? Is there anyone who only drinks scotch? Once you've found out everyone's proclivities, then whittle it down. Only one person drinks rye. Nix the rye. So-and-so drinks red wine but also drinks vodka and tonics. Nix the red wine. Exotic drinks are out. No piña coladas, no pineapple juice. Those drinks are good for other theme-specific parties. Also, drinks like Manhattans or martinis take time to make, so just concentrate on the drinks that are referred to as highballs: liquor plus mixer plus ice, or that come right out of the bottle: beer or wine. Start assembling your bar by thinking of it as five different pieces: (1) hard liquor, (2) beer and wine, (3) mixers, (4) ice, and (5) hardware. Also, buy more than you think you'll need. Nothing kills a party faster than running out of booze.

When you start to make your shopping list, first write out everything you'll need under each section without thinking of the amounts. For example, under hard liquor you'll need vodka, gin, tequila, and Scotch. Then prioritize each according to their popularity: 1. vodka, 2. tequila, 3. gin, 4. Scotch. From here, you can figure out how many bottles you need of each because you know that each bottle will produce about fifteen drinks. So you'll need six bottles of vodka since you estimate that one-third of your guests will be drinking vodka, three bottles of tequila, two of gin, and only one of Scotch. The rest of your gang drinks beer and wine.

There is a big debate about garnishes at a party of this size. Usually you cut up a bunch of limes, place them in a cute little bowl, and the next morning, besides finding a half dozen of them flattened on your floor, there's a cute little bowl on the bar filled with dried-out limes. It certainly is nice to offer a garnish, but it's up to you whether you want to make the effort.

For the beer, estimate that every beer drinker will have four. And you know there are ten people who drink only beer. So we'll need a minimum of two cases and probably three to be safe.

For the wine, you have a small portion of guests, probably five to seven. Figure one bottle per person, although you should get one case. It's a little cheaper, and you can always keep it in the fridge for future parties.

Mixers are tricky in that they are served both individually and in mixed drinks. The two mixers to stock up on are coke and club soda. The others will more than likely just be used in drinks. So get two of everything (one liter size) and four cokes and six club sodas.

Ice is a big neccesity, and although it is for the drinks, the bulk will be used to keep the beer cold in the bathtub. Order three thirty-pound bags. Two will be unloaded onto the beer in the tub, and the other will remain intact in the tub for refilling the ice bin by the bar.

The last section is one that gets most overlooked. This includes all the necessities for making your drinks and also keeping your bar tidy, which at about 2 A.M. is all but impossible. Here you must think of every gadget, glass, paper towel, can opener, and what have you that you will need throughout the

night. For the glasses, multiply the number of guests by three. Many guests will reuse their glasses, and some are drinking beer, so this has always been the right multiplier. For the other necessities, here's a list:

2 rolls of paper towels
2 can openers (one for beer the other for juice)
One ice bowl
Box of garbage bags
One wine opener

There's the basics for your bar. You might need to alter some things to suit your friends, like adding a bottle of bourbon or forgetting wine altogether. Just remember: a well-stocked bar today leads to happy hangovers tomorrow.

Miss Party Fabulous Says: Hire a bartender for the Studio 54 party. Make sure that he's got nice pecs and doesn't mind wearing silver lamé hot pants.

recipes

No slaving over a hot stove for this party. Find yourself a well-stocked candy store and go wild. Here are a few suggestions.

Good and Fruity	Candy cigarettes	Good & Plenty
Sweetarts	Blo Pops	Dots on paper
Candy necklaces	Wax lips	Zots
Gum, any kind	Red Hots	M&M's

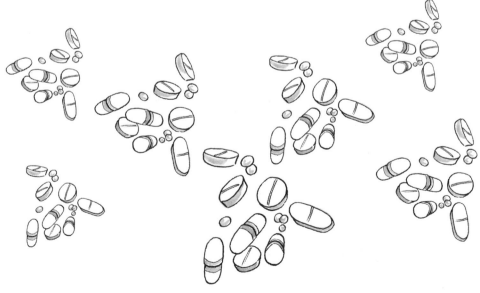

Mama Gawlikowski's Roadkill Polenta Party for Eight Intrepid Guests

MENU  Cheese Fondue with Mixed Vegetables and Breadsticks
Sage-Parmesan Polenta
Roadkill Ragout
Mixed Green Salad with Figs and Walnuts
Snowflake Sugar Cookies

GAMES AND THINGS Outdoor Activities
Group Ornament Making

COCKTAILS Manhattan

CRAFTS Snowy Snowy Invitation
Plain and Fancy Foil Wreaths

Wintertime

Wintertime means so many different things. A fire in the fireplace, a kiss under the mistletoe, a drink from a flask on the ski slopes, the bills after Christmas, a long depression in February . . . So many things! The magic begins with the first snowfall, and we've chosen a very special party to celebrate that very special day.

As soon as the leaves begin to change color and the air gets crisp, it's time to start preparations for Mama Gawlikowski's Roadkill Polenta Party. Send out the invitations, telling your prospective guests, "I don't know exactly when this party is going to be, but as soon as you see the first snowflake, expect a call from me." Prepare the stew and stow it away in your freezer. Even the dessert can be made ahead of time and frozen. Then, when the snow starts to fly, call up your comrades and tell them to come on over. Build a fire in the fireplace, defrost the stew, make the polenta, and celebrate the change of seasons while it's all still new and before cabin fever sets in.

When Mama Gawlikowski made her annual polenta feast, she used game that the menfolk had hunted down that fall, not roadkill. But just in case your menfolk came up short this year, and you find your supply of squirrel, possum, and bunny running low, just fire up the old station wagon and aim toward anything with four legs. But, seriously, where you get your meat is your own business, just take it

MAMA GAWLIKOWSKI'S ROADKILL POLENTA PARTY FOR EIGHT INTREPID GUESTS

from us: there is something special about game. The problem with society is we've all grown as complacent as the cows we eat. When you cook a wild thing, you can smell the mysteries of the forest emanating from your stove, and when you eat a wild thing, you can be certain some of its wildness will be parlayed to you. The flavor might be unfamiliar and somewhat stronger than what you're accustomed to, but that's the point. It's wild—and eating a wild thing is a much more exciting experience than eating a barnyard pig.

You'll want to plan an outdoor activity for before dinner. It can be anything from building a snowman to ice skating to caroling for your neighbors. When you've had enough of the winter wonderland, bring everyone back to your place and warm them up with some nice brown liquor and a nice fire in the fireplace. Put the winter records on, and get the guests started making Christmas ornaments for the tree while you finish preparing dinner. Then gather everyone up and slather the polenta and the stew right onto the table. While you're enjoying the fall's bounty, be thankful for the simple things, like a good snowfall and a good possum at the side of the road.

Miss Party Fabulous Says: Satanists, serial killers, psychopaths: They're your friends. Invite them.

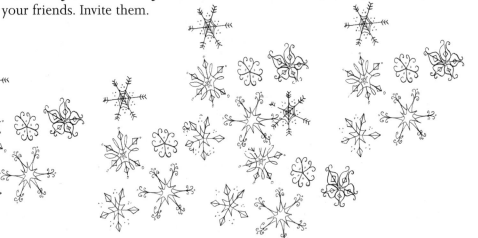

invitations

Snowy Snowy Invitation

This invitation is easy, but at the same time, it is time-consuming. Also, it has to be made so far in advance of the party that you might not have gotten in your Party Fabulous mode. Never mind; you've got to do it because you're planning a party.

YOU'LL NEED

Eight mini boxes of Snowy Bleach
A felt-tip pen
Scissors
White tape
Eight paper snowflakes
Scotch tape

- First, form a lovely relationship with the person who works at the local laundry. Laundry? Well, yes. The invitation is going to be printed on the back of the box of Snowy Bleach, and you can only get the mini ones at a laundromat. Having a friend at the laundromat who will save the empties for you will be most helpful.
- Once you've got those empties home, cut out the front of the boxes since we're going to make postcards.
- Tape a snowflake on the front.
- Border the card with the white tape to give it a lovely framed effect.

- Write all the party info on the back (make sure that you mention that the date of the party is when there is the first snowfall) along with your guest's address.
- Send them out in September (or August, if you live in the snow belt) to give yourself plenty of time before the first big snowfall.

Foil Wreaths

Can we talk about the wonder of aluminum foil for a moment? It's both cheap and easily manipulated, in addition to being shiny, beautiful, and silver. In your next life, pray to come back as a giant-sized roll of Reynolds Wrap.

There are several ways to make a foil wreath. We're going to focus on two: the easy way and the hard way. Whichever one you decide to do, take the advice of the Alcoa company (they're the people who bring you the lovely aluminum foil): "Think happy thoughts and your decorations will be beautiful."

EASY

YOU'LL NEED   One or two rolls of 12" wide foil
A bow
Whatever else you want to stick on it (ornaments, Christmas cards, some candles)
Pins or wires for attaching

- Just take your roll of foil and start molding it into a wreath, continuing around and adding layers until you get the size you desire (see figures 1 and 2).
- Once the wreath is the proper size, you can do any number of things with it.
- You can take some old ornaments and cover the wreath with them, using a pipe cleaner to attach each ornament to a stick that you will then insert into the wreath. Or attach your Christmas cards, using dressmaker's pins.
- Don't forget to tie a big bow to the top.
- One of the nicest ways to use this particular wreath is as a centerpiece. Lay it flat on the table and puncture holes in it, then insert candles all the way around.
- By the end of the party, you can be sure one of your guests will be donning your centerpiece on his head, thus becoming a flaming queen instead of a dancing queen.

Fig. 1

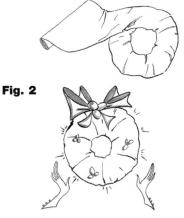

Fig. 2

MORE DIFFICULT   For all you advanced craftspeople, here's a variation on the foil wreath theme.

YOU'LL NEED   Four rolls of 12" wide aluminum foil
Florist tape or silver tape
Lightweight wire
One coat hanger
A big red bow

Fig. 1

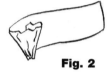

Fig. 2

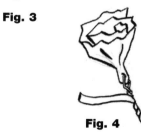

Fig. 3

Fig. 4

- Take each roll of foil and tear it into lengths of 20".
- Stack them, four layers per stack.
- Take each stack and cut it in half lengthwise, so that you now have rectangles that are 6" × 20" (fig. 1).
- Gather each stack into a series of tucks and pleats to form a rosette (fig. 2).
- Pierce the rosette with the lightweight wire, then wrap the wire around to form a stem 3" or 4" in length (fig. 3).
- Cover each stem with tape (fig. 4).
- When you are finished turning all the stacks of foil into lovely rosettes, take your coat hanger and shape it into a circle, leaving the hook intact at the top to hang it.
- Wrap each rosette onto the coat hanger frame, using more tape to secure it (fig. 5).
- Attach the big red bow at the top, using wire (fig. 6).
- Then sit back and admire your beautiful handiwork.

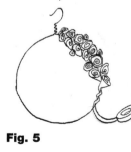

Fig. 5

Fig. 6

Outdoor Activities

We don't really go outside much, particularly when it's cold, so you're kind of on your own when it comes to this one. But from what we read, some people like to ski (downhill or cross-country), ice skate, sled, snowshoe, make snowmen, and have snowball fights when it snows. Pick one and try it—and be sure and let us know how it turns out.

Group Ornament Making

This is a free-for-all activity, with no set instructions. As the host/ess, all you do is set out the provisions and let the guests do the work. The following is a list of some of the things you might include:

Scissors
Glue
Tape (in addition to clear tape, you might include different colors to use as decoration)
Stapler
Colored markers
Ruler
Construction paper
Cardboard
Origami paper
Scraps of wrapping paper
Scraps of fabric
Ribbon
Macaroni in various shapes

Ornament hooks
Wire
Toothpicks
Old Christmas cards
Magazines
Glitter
Yarn
Dime store toys and figurines, particularly ones with a holiday motif
Paper plates
Small boxes

Just to get you started, here's one of our favorite holiday decorations, a macaroni wreath.

YOU'LL NEED   Medium-weight cardboard
Glue
Macaroni in various shapes, such as shells, rigatoni, wheels, etc.
Gold spray paint
Thick red yarn

- Draw a circle, 6" in diameter, on your cardboard.
- Cut out.
- Draw a second circle, 1½" in diameter at the center of your cardboard circle.
- Cut this out, using an X-Acto knife.
- You now have a cardboard doughnut, but for our purposes, it's a wreath.
- Make a puncture hole at the top of your wreath—that's where you'll hang it from later.
- Cover your wreath with glue, and squeeze an extra puddle of glue on a saucer for dipping purposes.
- Now take the macaroni and dip each piece into the glue puddle, then stick it onto the wreath.
- Continue this process until every millimeter of the wreath is covered with macaroni.
- Leave to dry.
- When dry, spray with gold spray paint.
- Thread the yarn through the hole, tie in a big bow, and hang from the tree.

Peggy Lee
A Natural Woman
Capitol Records

Walt Disney's *Bambi* (as
dramatized by Shirley
Temple)
RCA Camden, 1960

The Dean Martin Christmas Album
Reprise Records
**"Let It Snow! Let It Snow!
Let It Snow!"**

Smokey Robinson and
The Miracles
The Season for Miracles
Motown Records, 1970
**"I Can Tell When Christmas
Is Near"**

Sammy Davis, Jr.
*A Live Performance of His
Greatest Hits*
Warner Bros. Records, 1977
"Talk to The Animals"

Roger Miller
Golden Hits
Smash Records
"King of the Road"

The Three Suns
The Sounds of Christmas
RCA Victor, 1955

Dave Brubeck's Greatest Hits
Columbia
"Take Five"

Fred Waring and the
Pennsylvanians
A Caroling We Go
MCA Records
"Caroling, Caroling"

Captain & Tenille's Greatest Hits
A&M Records, 1977
"Muscrat Love"

Buffy Sainte-Marie
*I'm Gonna Be a Country Girl
Again*
Vanguard
**"Now That the Buffalo's
Gone"**

M'm! M'm! Good!
Columbia Records
Featuring Lester Lanin
" M'm! M'm! Good!"

cocktails

Manhattan

When the weather outside is frightful and you've been playing in it, you need a drink that will warm you from the top of your head to the tips of your toes. Now, you're probably thinking that a hot drink is what's called for. Wrong, wrong, wrong. Hot drinks make you sleepy. What you need is something that heats you up with its magical chemistry, not with its temperature. And what might that be? Well, my liquor instincts tell me that a little brown liquor is just what's needed. Why not a Manhattan? No rocks—just straight up.

Mmmmmm. That first sip doesn't even make it to your tummy. It just courses through your body, waking up all those little nerve endings that thought they had given themselves up to frostbite. We might just mix up a batch right this minute—and it's not even winter!

YOU'LL NEED

A bottle of bourbon (Wild Turkey of course, you will be eating game, after all)
A bottle of sweet vermouth
Maraschino cherries

In a shaker, put some ice. Add about four parts of bourbon to one part vermouth. You can make the drink drier or sweeter by the amount of vermouth you put in. Give it a couple of stirs, then strain into a martini glass. Add a maraschino cherry, and you've got a down comforter in a glass.

HOT AFTER DINNER DRINKS

Hold it right there! You're not finished yet! Now that dinner's over, this is the time for those lovely hot drinks. Something with hot chocolate or warm apple cider. You've already got the bourbon and that would be delish with the cider or since you've already been eating maraschinos, some cherry liqueur would be good with the hot chocolate. Whichever you decide, nap time is just around the corner—and your dreams are certain to be sweet.

recipes

Cheese Fondue with Mixed Vegetables and Breadsticks

The weather outside might be frightful, but this dish is delightful! So, clear the cobwebs off that old fondue pot, polish it up, and let's have some fun. Have your vegetables steamed and cheese grated ahead of time, so that when you come in from the great outdoors this starter should take you only ten minutes to prepare.

1 qt. white wine
1 tablespoon garlic, minced
1 teaspoon red pepper flakes
2 tablespoons cornstarch
2 tablespoons cold water

1 cup Swiss cheese, grated
1 cup Gruyère cheese
1 cup Parmesan cheese, grated
1 cup Fontina cheese, grated

Bring wine, garlic, and red pepper flakes to a boil.

While the wine is heating up, make a cornstarch paste by dissolving the cornstarch into the cold water. Set aside.

When the wine begins to boil, gradually add all of the cheeses. Once the cheese has melted, whisk in the cornstarch paste. Lower to medium heat and continue stirring for one more minute. Be careful not to let the fondue boil, or mixture will separate.

Transfer to fondue pot over medium heat and start dipping.

THE VEGETABLES

2 heads of broccoli, flowerets	4 carrots, sliced
2 heads of cauliflower, flowerets	2 lb. asparagus, peeled
2 large potatoes, cubed	Breadsticks

All vegetables should be bite-size.

You'll need a pot for boiling water and a bamboo steamer that fits onto this pot. Bring water to a boil and steam vegetables, one type at a time, for about 3 to 5 minutes or until tender. When steamed, remove vegetables and shock them in a pan of ice water. Drain and pat dry. This will help retain the vegetables' vibrant colors. Wrap vegetables and refrigerate until ready to serve.

Arrange on large platter, alternating vegetables with breadsticks.

Sage-Parmesan Polenta

This party has the potential to become a treasured annual tradition, if global warming doesn't eliminate snowfall completely. At this party, dinner is literally served on the table—no centerpiece, no plates, just a table covered with aluminum foil onto which the polenta is poured and covered with the game ragout. All you need to set for this one is a fork, knife, napkin, and a steady flow of wine.

By all means, don't prepare this dinner on your prized polished antique cherry drop leaf that's been handed down through generations. A large Formica-topped kitchen table will do just fine.

6 qt. milk	3 cups Parmesan cheese, grated
1 lb. butter	3 bunches sage, chopped
8 lb. instant yellow Polenta	Salt and pepper
4 qt. water	

Combine the milk, butter and water in a medium to large pot and bring to a boil. Whisk in the Polenta, stirring constantly until mixture bubbles. Reduce heat. Stir in cheese, sage, and season with salt and pepper. Remove from heat and let cool slightly. Pour the thick polenta onto a table that is covered with aluminum foil. Shape polenta so that it's about 1" thick with a slight lip around the edge to hold the ragout. As it cools, it should set so that you can cut it with a knife. Dig in!

Miss Party Fabulous Says: If you have any left-over Polenta, cut it into squares and wrap with foil used to cover the table. Let your guests take some home—delicious hot or cold as a midday snack.

Roadkill Ragout

1 cup olive oil
1 cup flour
Salt and pepper
3 osso buco (veal shank),
    center cut, 1½" thick
2 rabbits, quartered
2 lb. venison leg, 2" cubes
2 lb. hot Italian sausage links
16 meatballs
1 large Spanish onion, diced

2 carrots, diced
2 celery stalks, diced
2 tablespoons garlic, minced
1 tablespoon red pepper flakes
1 qt. red wine
1 bunch rosemary
1 bunch thyme
1 bunch sage
2 #10 cans (approx. 6 qt.)
    plum tomatoes

In a large stockpot with a thick bottom, heat the olive oil to a point when the oil starts to smoke.

Season flour with salt and pepper. Flour the osso buco, rabbit, and venison. Brown each piece on both sides, about 2 minutes per side. Remove from oil and set aside. Brown the sausage and meatballs for about 2 minutes. Remove from oil and set aside. Add the onions, carrots, celery, garlic, and pepper flakes. Sauté for 5 to 7 minutes or until brown. To this add the wine, herbs, tomatoes, and all of the meats and their juices. Reduce heat to simmer and cook for 4½ hours. With a slotted spoon, remove all meat and bones. Remove meat from bones. Set aside. Return bones to sauce and reduce at high heat for about ½ hour. Skin all fat from the top of sauce. Strain sauce through a sieve and puree with stick blender. Return meat to sauce and season with salt and pepper. When polenta is arranged on table, ladle just enough sauce to cover the polenta. Arrange meat evenly over polenta and pour remaining sauce into bowl to serve on the side. Also have some extra Parmesan on hand.

THE MEATBALLS

1 lb. ground beef	2 teaspoons oregano
1 lb. ground pork	2 teaspoons thyme
1 lb. ground veal	2 teaspoons basil
8 eggs	2 tablespoons garlic, minced
2 cups bread crumbs, plain	1 bunch parsley, chopped
2 tablespoons sugar	Salt and pepper

In a large mixing bowl, combine all ingredients. Add a generous pinch of salt and pepper. Form mixture into 16 large meatballs. When rolling meatballs, sprinkle a bit of water on your palms to keep meat from sticking to your hands.

Mixed Green Salad with Figs and Walnuts

This simple salad can be served on a platter set in the middle of the table around which the polenta is poured. Or you can serve it on salad plates. Whichever way you go, be sure to eat with your fingers.

1 head escarole	Vinaigrette dressing
1 head chicory	Salt and pepper
¼ head red cabbage	1 pt. figs, quartered
2 heads radicchio	¼ cup walnuts, chopped

Thoroughly wash all greens, spin dry, and tear into bite-size pieces. Mix greens in a bowl and toss with vinaigrette. Season with salt and pepper. Transfer to platter and garnish with figs and walnuts.

VINAIGRETTE DRESSING

6 oz. extra-virgin olive oil	1 teaspoon oregano
2 oz. red wine vinegar	Salt and pepper

In a small bowl, mix all ingredients. Season with salt and pepper. Toss with greens.

Snowflake Sugar Cookies

¾ cup pine nuts, toasted
¼ lb. unsalted butter
½ cup sugar
1 cup all-purpose flour, sifted

2 egg yolks
1 teaspoon lemon zest
1 teaspoon orange zest
Optional: 1 tablespoon Amaretto

Preheat oven to 350°. Toast pine nuts on a cookie sheet for 3 to 4 minutes. Set aside.

In a medium bowl, cream butter and sugar together until smooth. Mix in all remaining ingredients except ¼ cup pine nuts to use as garnish. If you want to add the amaretto, pour it in now.

On a lightly floured surface, roll out dough, cut into 1" balls, and flatten. Place cookies on a greased and lightly floured cookie sheet, 2" apart. Arrange those extra pine nuts on top of cookies.

Bake for 20 to 25 minutes.

Set aside and let cool on rack.

Breakfast at Tiffany's
(A "Let's Dress Up and Act Like Adults" Party for as Many People as You Can Find)

MENU
Olives Stuffed with Tuna
Salami Horns
Cherry Tomatoes with Egg Salad and Caviar
Sweet Sausage and Peppers in Puff Pastry
Dates Stuffed with Marscapone and Pistachios
Four A.M. Egg Supreme
Holly's Home Fries

GAMES AND THINGS
Breakfast at Tiffany's Playhouse
Get the Guest

COCKTAILS
Martini

CRAFTS
Holly Golightly Invitation

This is either the easiest or the hardest party. It's the easiest because there isn't a lot of preparation but the hardest because you have to rely on the social skills you've been developing over the last eleven parties. This one isn't about crafts or games, it's about smoking and drinking. It should start in a dignified place, then spiral downward into a drunken stupor. Dress up like the adult you thought you'd grow up to be when you were a little kid.

Here are a few tidbits to remember to help set this party off and make it a big, *Breakfast at Tiffany's*–style blowout, and not just another drab, blasé cocktail party.

The guests. Invite the most interesting people you know, and then send them each five or so extra invitations so that they, in turn, can invite the most interesting people they know. Think Holly Golightly. Remember how she lit up when Rusty Trawler came in the door, because she immediately knew that he was the "ninth richest man in the United States under the age of fifty"? Well, you should be so smart. Make sure that there are at least four or five people at the party that you want to get to know better for one reason or another: the cute boy from the country club or the cute girl at the gas station. Invite them both.

Plenty of liquor. This time, we mean it. Estimate what you need, then double that amount.

The music. We tried to play only the sound track from *Breakfast at Tiffany's* and other similar cocktail-type music, but there were protests. Instead, you might want to keep a carefully chosen assortment of albums near the turntable and do the DJ routine, mixing "I Love the Nightlife" with a good cha-cha number.

Bowls of cigarettes.

The delivery. In the movie, the best part of the party scene is when the liquor arrives and Holly yells, "Reenforcements!!" For your party, it doesn't necessarily have to be alcohol, it can be a pizza or twenty extra-large orders of fries from McDonald's or ice or even Dial-A-Mattress. Just make sure that the delivery person walks through the entire party, and make him stay for at least one cocktail.

It doesn't hurt if you or someone else does the best Holly Golightly. You know, bouffant hairdo and cocktail dress, cigarette holder. This someone should be there to break the ice between strangers and lead the conga line up to the roof.

You. Dress fabulously. Be your most witty and charming. Save up your most fabulous cocktail party anecdotes for the occasion. Be yourself, but be *fabulous*.

And remember, it isn't a real *Breakfast at Tiffany's* Party unless someone yells, "Tim-berr!!!"

Miss Party Fabulous Suggests: If you're throwing a martini-only party, 40 pounds of ice will do. If you're going to do beer, too, start with about 120 pounds (yes!) of ice. About 90 pounds of this will go in your bathtub to chill beer, etc.

Keep the coats in the bedroom. (Make sure you make the bed!) Start the first coats at the headboard and progress to the footboard, then start a new layer at the headboard again. If you have one person in charge of this, he'll have to be able to help guests when they want to leave.

Don't forget to invite the neighbors. You don't want any Mr. Yunioski on your hands!

Change your maid's housecleaning day to the day after the party, but be sure she doesn't come until after noon (or even 3:00 P.M.!)

Put anything breakable or valuable in the cellar or the attic or your neighbor's apartment.

Holly Golightly Invitation

The design for this invitation is going to have the feel of a business card. After all, Holly was a self-employed working girl and needed to get her name out.

YOU'LL NEED

One Sheet of paper
Felt-tip pen
Ruler

- If you have a computer that has a business card template, that is fabulous. If you don't, never mind; you can size it out on a piece of paper.
- Measure out a rectangle at the top left corner of your paper that measures 2" × 3½".
- Using your felt-tip pen, write out the info for the party, arranging it so that it has the look of a business card.
- The invitation should read: Holly Golightly invites you to a drinks party for The honorable Blah, Blah, Blah (make up any name), Esq. Put a lot of those honorable and Esq. things in so everyone thinks they're going to a real fancy-shmancy party.
- Also, put a little drawing of a martini glass in the corner or a cigarette in a cigarette holder to give your invitees a small hint of what's to come.
- After the original of the card is done, you're going to need to go to the copier or a copy machine (the office copy machine would work, but don't get caught).

- Make copies and then cut and paste so that you then have a full sheet of paper covered in Holly business cards.
- Now you need to actually go to the copy store. Have them copy your sheet onto—Are you ready?—Tiffany Blue card stock. Then have them cut them for you.
- Since you're going to invite just about everyone in the known world to this party, keep a bunch of them on your person to hand out all over town.

Breakfast at Tiffany's Playhouse

At this party, we think it's kind of fun to act out your favorite scenes. You can do this any number of ways. For instance, you can just pick a character and improvise as that character all night long. It might be something as simple as deciding you're OJ Vermin, in which case you'd just call everyone Fred baby or Johnny baby all night long. You might confuse some friends who don't have a clue as to what you're doing, but that's okay. Even if they don't understand it, they might end up playing along, anyway. Or you can just act out bits, such as lighting someone's hat on fire with a cigarette, then putting it out with a cocktail. Or laughing hysterically into the mirror, then suddenly weeping uncontrollably.

Another way to do it is to transcribe a few scenes from the movie, photocopy them, then leave them lying around. Instead of trying to get all the guests involved in this activity, you'll find that small groups will gravitate to it, acting out scenes around the kitchen table or in the bedroom, lying on the bed on top of all the coats.

An easier way to do this is to buy a few copies of the book (Yes, darling, it was a *book* before it became a movie.) and highlight the segments that lend themselves to playacting.

We had loads of fun acting out the party scene at our *Breakfast at Tiffany's* party. It created a party within a party, a meta-party. The only downside was that *everyone* thinks they're born to play Holly.

Get the Guest   We think you all probably know how to play this game. It's something that comes naturally sometimes, after a few too many cocktails, when you can no longer conceal the bitchiness that resides under the surface. This game is for when *Breakfast at Tiffany's* disintegrates into *Who's Afraid of Virginia Woolf?*

Pick a guest—any guest. Gang up on him/her. Tell him all those things you've been dying to tell him, about how he always calls at the wrong time, overstays his welcome, is an incurable cheapskate/alcoholic/slut. You get the idea. You may be shattering your friend's ego, but in your heart you believe that it is all for his own good. After all, it's important for him to know the truth, and there's no one who can tell the truth and shame the devil like you.

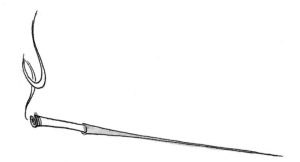

Breakfast at Tiffany's
Sound Track
RCA Victor, 1961

Let's Dance with the Three Suns
RCA Victor, 1958
"I Love Paris"

Al Ciaola
Ciao
United Artists Records
"Quando, Quando, Quando"

Burt Bacharach
Reach Out
A&M Records
**"What the World Needs
Now is Love"**

Ethel Smith
Latin from Manhattan
Decca Records
"Tico Tico"

Petula Clark
I Know a Place
Warner Bros. Records
"The 'In' Crowd"

Dance Party, Volume I
Pickwick International
"Perfidia" (Rumba)

Something's Cookin
The Fired up Howard
Robert's Quartet—with
Brass
Capitol Records
"Charade"

*Herb Alpert Presents Sergio
Mendez and Brazil 66*
A&M Records
"Going out of My Head"

Bent Fabric
Alley Cat
Atco Records, 1962
"Catsanova Walk"

Sylvia deSayles
The Best Is Yet to Come
Regina Records
"Married I Can Always Get"

Eydie Gourmet
I Feel So Spanish
United Artists
"Never on Sunday"

cocktails

Martini

Think back. When you were a kid, what drink did you think was desperately chic, terribly adult. The drink that you knew that if you were allowed to have one, you would be a grown-up. Never mind that at the time it actually tasted like jet fuel. You had to have one. And after the adults gave you a sip, you made one of those horrible faces like a scary shrunken apple head while they lit into peals of laughter. And you vowed, "One Day." Well, that day is here. It's time for a Party Fabulous martini! There are zillions of specialty martinis out there: sakitinis, peartinis, every kind of flavored vodkatinis—but for our Party Fabulous, we're going to stick with the semi-traditional vodka martini. It's only semi-traditional, because we're not going to use gin or the classic amount of dry vermouth, which way back when, was a third of the drink.

YOU'LL NEED

Lots of chilled vodka (brand is definitely up to you, everyone has their preference)
Two bottles of dry vermouth (amount really depends on the amount of people who are coming to the party, but 2 should more than cover 100)
600 cocktail olives (3 to a drink, so that's 2 drinks apiece for 100 revelers)

For this party, we'll make pitchers of martinis, unless you want to hire a bunch of bartenders who will make them individually, nonstop, for the duration of the party. Pitchers it is. The vodka should be bought a few days in advance and stocked in your freezer. A good-sized freezer can hold about sixteen bottles, which should get you started. Fill your pitchers about a third of the way with ice (because the vodka has been in the freezer a few days, you don't want too much; besides, you don't want your martinis to become too diluted). Pour in a shot of dry vermouth and swish it around. Then strain it out. Now the vermouth is coated on the ice and the sides of the pitcher. Now fill it up with vodka. Give it a couple of stirs and pour into those classic martini glasses with three olives. Actually, you'll probably be pouring them into little plastic cups. Who has martini glasses for 100? And there you go. Someone will be yelling, "*Timber!*" any minute.

TIMBER!

Olives Stuffed with Tuna

3 lb. imported tuna in olive oil	3 tablespoons capers
Dash of lime juice	Pepper to taste
1 cup celery, chopped	100 large pitted Sicilian olives
1 cup red onion, chopped	Pimiento, diced

In a food processor, mix tuna (drained), lime juice, celery, onion, capers, and pepper. Puree until smooth. Using a pastry bag, pipe filling into olives. Garnish olives with a sprinkle of pimiento.

Arrange olives in small Tiffany boxes on tray.

Salami Horns

2½ cups sun-dried tomatoes	1 teaspoon garlic, chopped
3 bunches basil	2 lb. Genoa salami, thinly sliced
2 lb. cream cheese, soft	Salt and pepper

Boil sun-dried tomatoes for 5 minutes. Drain and set aside.

Rinse basil. Set aside. In a food processor, combine the cream cheese, garlic, tomatoes, and 2 bunches of basil. Puree until smooth. Season with salt and pepper. Set aside.

Make one cut in each piece of salami from the center to the outer edge. Roll into a horn.

Using a pastry bag, pipe filling into horn. Spear with frilly toothpick and garnish with basil leaf.

Arrange on long, oval tray to spell out *Holly!*

Cherry Tomatoes with Egg Salad and Caviar

5 pints cherry tomatoes
12 eggs, hard-boiled
2 cups mayonnaise
1 bunch chives
2 tablespoons Worcestershire sauce

3 tablespoons cider vinegar
2 tablespoons dry mustard
Salt, to taste
2 teaspoons white pepper
5 oz. black lumpfish caviar

Use a sharp paring knife and slice the top of each tomato. Scoop out center of tomato. Slice a small piece off bottom of tomato, to place standing on tray.

In a food processor, blend the eggs, mayonnaise, chives, Worcestershire, vinegar, mustard, salt, and pepper.

You can either use a pastry bag and pipe filling into tomatoes or use a melon baller and stuff tomatoes.

Garnish with a sprinkle of caviar.

Arrange tomatoes in small Tiffany boxes on trays.

Sweet Sausage and Peppers in Puff Pastry

7 lb. sweet Italian sausage links
10 red peppers, diced
3 oz. olive oil

10 eggs
5 sheets 8" × 12" puff pastry
1 cup black poppy seeds

Preheat oven to 450°. Roast sausage for 15 minutes. Let cool, transfer to a clean pan, and refrigerate. When sausage is cold, slice and set aside.

Rinse, seed, and dice red peppers. In a sauté pan, heat the olive oil and sauté red peppers for 5 minutes. Set aside.

In a small bowl, beat the eggs. Set aside.

Lay out sheets of pastry and cut out 2" rounds.

To assemble, place a piece of sausage on pastry round. Sprinkle with red peppers. Cover with another pastry round, and crimp edges with a fork. Brush top of pastry with egg wash. Garnish with sprinkle of poppy seeds.

Reduce oven to 400°. Bake for 10 to 12 minutes or until pastry is golden brown.

Arrange on long, oval tray to spell out *Cat!*

Serve with a small dish of whole-grain mustard.

Dates Stuffed with Marscapone and Pistachios

50 dried dates, pitted
2 qt. marscapone
1 tablespoon black pepper

2 lb. cream cheese
1 lb. pistachios, chopped

Cut dates in half lengthwise. Set aside.

In a bowl, cream together the marscapone, pepper, and cream cheese.

Using a pastry bag, pipe filling into dates.

Garnish with a sprinkle of pistachio.

Four A.M. Egg Supreme

Just before sunrise, pop into the kitchen and start your egg supreme. Tempt that old gang that's always the last to leave into the kitchen for some breakfast. Mix up some Bloody Marys, throw open the windows, let the sunshine in, and gather everyone around the table. A perfect ending to a perfect party.

8 dozen eggs	2 bunches chives, chopped
1 lb. unsalted butter	Toast
2 lb. smoked salmon	

Remove eggs from shells. Discard shells. In a bowl, beat 2 dozen eggs until smooth.

In a large Teflon pan, melt ¼ pound of butter. When butter begins to bubble, add eggs. Stir with rubber spatula. Depending on your preference, scramble eggs for 1 to 3 minutes. When eggs look good, fold in ½ pound of smoked salmon and some chives. Serve with buttered toast. Repeat as needed.

HOLLY'S HOME FRIES

A delicious accompaniment to eggs supreme. The beauty of this recipe is that you can bake the potatoes the day before your party, leaving you with a few simple steps to follow at sunrise.

10 large Idaho potatoes
½ cup canola oil
salt and pepper to taste

The day before:
Preheat oven to 400°. Thoroughly scrub and dry potatoes. Bake for 45 minutes. The potatoes will not be fully cooked, as you are going to pan fry them later. Wrap and refrigerate overnight.

End of the party:
Preheat oven to 400°. When ready to make home fries peel potatoes, and using a cheese grater (the side with the largest holes) grate potatoes. Season with salt and pepper.
In a cast iron pan, add enough oil to cover bottom of pan. Heat oil and then fill pan ¾ full with grated potatoes. Reduce heat and brown potatoes for 2 minutes. Carefully flip "pancake" and brown other side for 2 minutes.
Place pan in oven and bake for 15 minutes. Transfer to plate and cut into quarters. Repeat process as needed.

fabulous!

1. Even though we don't adhere to this ourselves, *plan ahead*.
2. Always flail your arms and exclaim the name of whoever is coming through the door.
3. "Take a picture—it'll last longer," is the motto of a friend of ours, and he's right. Don't just take one, take lots of pictures at each of your parties, then invite everyone back a week or two later to see them. The party never stops with this fail-proof method.
4. Figure out how much liquor you need, then double it. What you think is too much is not enough.
5. Eat beforehand.

Remember

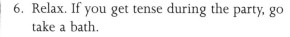

6. Relax. If you get tense during the party, go take a bath.
7. Make extra—for all those extra people.
8. Remember, you never really know if you had a good time until the next day when you're discussing the whole thing on the phone with your best friend. Even dismal parties can end up seeming okay in the reviewing process.
9. Buy a brand-new needle for the phonograph, and do a little sound check in advance.
10. Keep an account with the florist to send some "I'm sorry" bouquets to the neighbors.